To Madi and Scout and all the daughters and sons
who have shared this path with me,

To my mother, who first introduced me
to the joy and comfort of reading,

To Cheryl and Peter, for showing me
teaching at its finest,

And to all our cherished authors
whose words have changed us forever.

Contents

"This powerful, moving collection offers a stunning reminder of how deeply young people are marked by books—how words can print themselves directly onto our hearts."

—Gayle Brandeis, author of *My Life with the Lincolns* and Bellwether Prize–winning *The Book of Dead Birds*

Bookmarked

Teen Essays on Life and Literature from Tolkien to Twilight

Edited by Ann Camacho

free spirit
PUBLISHING®

Library of Congress Cataloging-in-Publication Data
Bookmarked : teen essays on life and literature from Tolkien to Twilight / edited by Ann Camacho.
   p. cm.
Includes index.
ISBN 978-1-57542-396-8
1. Literature—Appreciation. 2. Teenagers—Books and reading. 3. Literature and morals. 4. Life in literature. I. Camacho, Ann.
PN47.B56 2012
809—dc23   2011043942

ISBN: 978-1-57542-396-8

Reading Level Grades 9 & up; Interest Level Ages 13 & up;
Fountas & Pinnell Guided Reading Level Z+

Edited by Alison Behnke
Cover and interior design by Michelle Lee Lagerroos
Poem from "When the Light Turns Blue" (pages 141–143) Copyright © 1981 EVIL EYE MUSIC, LLC. Used by permission of HarperCollins Publishers.

10 9 8 7 6 5 4 3
Printed in the United States of America
S13971015

Free Spirit Publishing Inc.
6325 Sandburg Road, Suite 100
Golden Valley, MN 55427-3629
(612) 338-2068
help4kids@freespirit.com
www.freespirit.com

Printed on
recycled paper

including 30%
post-consumer waste

"You are braver than you believe, stronger than you seem, and smarter than you think."

—Christopher Robin in A.A. Milne's *Winnie the Pooh*

Introduction

Has a phrase from a book, an idea from a story, or a verse from a poem ever crept into your soul, left a mark on your heart, or changed your life?

Two years ago, I was reading a book that changed *my* life. It was a collection of essays about people's beliefs: beliefs about life, about love, about themselves and the world. These essays were sometimes inspiring and sometimes sad. But most of all, they were inviting. They invited and challenged me to look at what my own most important belief might be, a single conviction that helped guide my life.

As I read, I realized that I already knew exactly what that single conviction was. As a high school English teacher, I talk to teens every day about the plots of books, about what happens in stories. I talk about characters and what they are going through, how they feel about their circumstances, their choices, and their lives. I know that many of my students—like you, perhaps—have looked at literature as a mandatory rigor in the educational path instead of a valued tool. However, my students could tell you that in my classroom I challenge this opinion, because what I *really* teach is my belief, my conviction: Books are blueprints for living and roadmaps for our lives.

After seeing this conviction clearly as I read that life-changing book of essays late one night, I sat straight up in bed. I was invigorated by a single idea. I wanted to learn more about how literature and reading had affected the lives and beliefs of my students. And then I wanted to share their stories with you—with other readers and other young people far and wide. Excited by this idea, I decided to reach out to my students, past and present. Below is an excerpt from my invitation to them:

> It's time your voice was heard; it is time your story was told. It is now your opportunity to share who you are. And it is your chance to give back to those who are on the same path that you've traveled. In a collection of essays . . . each of you will have this opportunity to leave your mark as authors have done before you. . . . Find a quote from ANY book you've read . . . and use it as the foundation or seed to developing your personal philosophy about how you live your life.

After sending out this invitation, I didn't know exactly what would happen next. What *did* happen was astonishing. Dozens of essays began pouring in. Many of the students who responded had faced and overcome incredible challenges, and all had interesting stories to tell. Each essay was striking in its own way, and each voice was amazingly unique and honest. As more and more essays showed up in my inbox, I knew I'd sparked a fire of self-reflection and personal insight.

The young people who wrote the essays in *Bookmarked* have laid out their fears, hopes, dreams, and experiences. I hope that, through their stories, you can find insight into your own life, making connections with other people as well as gathering personal strength and wisdom. These student writers have bright futures, but their paths have not necessarily been smooth or without hardship. They have learned much and they have wisdom to share, just as you do.

And they've discovered—as you may have—that books can leave a mark on our lives, an imprint that changes us forever. Oxford professor and author of the Chronicles of Narnia series, C.S. Lewis, once said, "We read to know we are not alone," and I hold his statement to be true. We read to know we are not going through this life without others who have also experienced some of what we are going through. We read to know there is guidance for our lives, a well-worn path that another has walked. We read to become better people, and we read because words have the power to change our lives. Books can tell us who we are and who we aren't—or, at least, who we don't want to be—both as individuals and as a society. They give us a chance to connect with others, and they build bridges between us and the world outside. Books can fill the emptiness and, if we let them, can replace our arrogance and selfishness with understanding and compassion. They teach us about our mistakes, they speak to us about difficult situations, and they remind us that we are not alone. From *Goodnight Moon* to *The Great Gatsby*, from sacred books to spiritual texts, and from Tolkien to *Twilight*, books mark our lives—and they help us leave our own mark on the world. What will yours be?

The essays in *Bookmarked* are grouped into five parts, each one exploring a big idea or theme that also appears in literature. Like the writers of these essays, you may find that words from literature can change or expand the way you think about these ideas—about your life, yourself, and your world. At the end of each part of the book, you'll find a section titled "And So . . . Questions for Writing, Reflection, and Discussion." The prompts in these sections can serve as guideposts as you explore the ideas in the essays. Use the questions in whatever way you like. You can reflect on them by yourself, talk about them with others, or do some writing of your own. If you decide to put your thoughts down on paper, try not to edit yourself or judge your own thoughts. Just start writing, no matter how it sounds in your head or how it appears on the page. Let your reactions and reflections pour forth.

If you want to share these reflections, or if you have other stories and thoughts about reading, writing, or how books have marked *your* life, I'd love to hear them. And if this book inspires you to write your own personal essay, I'd love to read it. You can email me at help4kids@freespirit .com, leave a comment on the *Bookmarked* blog at bookmarkedteens.net, or write to me in care of the following address:

Free Spirit Publishing
217 Fifth Avenue North, Suite 200
Minneapolis, MN 55401-1299

And so, I wish for you what I wish for my students: a foundation of truth and insight, and the chance to anchor your life, in some way, through this and any other book that you encounter along your path. Remember, you are not alone!

Ann Camacho

Part 1
Essays on Beliefs and Ideals

"All we have to decide is what to do
with the time that is given us."
—Gandalf in J.R.R. Tolkien's *The Fellowship of the Ring*

No Royal Road

by Karisa Booth

Today, with all the new technology that is constantly being introduced, it is sometimes hard to keep the purpose of an education in perspective. I feel that my generation, if given a choice, will always take the easy way out. After all, more often than not, we have more machines, more technology, and more people doing the work for us than earlier students ever had. While I don't mean to discredit the advancement of society, I think there is something to be said about accomplishing work that is mentally or physically demanding and the intrinsic reward it has to offer.

But being of this generation, I do find myself looking for that shortcut, that way "out," so that I can do what I feel is more important or more interesting or simply more what I want to do. I forget that it is the process of learning something new that gives me true joy.

In one of my classes in college, I was supposed to read *Barchester Towers* by Anthony Trollope, but like many busy (and lazy) college students, I used SparkNotes instead. On SparkNotes, I discovered an important message in the author's words. He wrote that "there is no royal road to learning; no short cut to the acquirement of any art." At the time, the author's words gave me no great epiphany. I continued to use SparkNotes for that project and never even bought the book for the class. That summer, after I had passed the class and the syllabus had been thrown away, I was browsing in the bookstore and stumbled across *Barchester Towers*. In class, it had sounded interesting, and now that I had some time on my hands, I decided to read it. I came across those words again, but this time, I decided to copy that quote and keep it on my wall to remind me that there are no shortcuts to learning. The process of doing the work and learning how to do the work is as valuable, if not more valuable, than the skill learned.

I thought back to third grade, remembering when we had to learn long division, which seemed rather ridiculous when we all had calculators. But there was something to be said about the importance of not only knowing the answer but also being able to solve a problem independent of outside assistance, whether it came from another person or the latest technology.

I've also come to realize that learning is not just done in the classroom; there is much to learn in life. I have now opened myself to learning about other cultures. Though I could take the easier way out and simply read books on ethnography and different cultures, I have chosen to experience the culture for myself. Today I am in Israel, lighting the menorah and saying the Hebrew prayers with my new friends here, prayers that have been said for thousands of years. I have seen that each experience in life comes with its own set of challenges, and I've definitely taken some short-cuts in my learning in the past. But I know now that there is more to learn about myself and my abilities when I take the long way around and do the work. It is the difference between taking the highway or the back roads. The trip is so much longer, but the views are so much better!

Karisa was born in Southern California to her amazingly support-ive parents. In May 2011, she graduated cum laude from George Washington University with degrees in geography and international affairs, with a concentration in international development. She now works at KaBOOM!, a nonprofit organization dedicated to saving play for kids in the United States.

Our Choices

by Raymond Yeung

Every life begins with a foundation. Each of us is born with our socioeconomic and cultural status already in place for us. Surely, growing up in that atmosphere may influence our dispositions, our goals, and even our successes and failures. However, do we also have choices? Can we determine our future through our own actions and opinions, or has our fate already been decided from the start?

In J.K. Rowling's second installment of the Harry Potter series, *Harry Potter and the Chamber of Secrets,* Harry ponders a similar question. He struggles with his placement in the Gryffindor house, believing that he had only been put in Gryffindor because of his continual pleas, despite having qualities that might otherwise have placed him in Slytherin. In response to Harry's question, Albus Dumbledore reassures the boy, "It is our choices, Harry, that show what we truly are, far more than our abilities." I couldn't agree more.

My mother was born in Vietnam and my father was born in Hong Kong. Both of my parents lived the majority of their lives in Hong Kong prior to coming to the United States more than 25 years ago. My father came to the United States in order to get an education. My grandfather from my mother's side was a Vietnamese refugee who escaped to the United States following the communist invasion of Vietnam. Meanwhile, my mother and other family members fled to Hong Kong and eventually rejoined my grandfather in the States. My parents chose to come to the United States for freedom, education, and possibilities of a bright future.

My parents' decision to leave Hong Kong and everything they knew in order to push through thickets of uncertainty in hopes of reaching the American Dream is characteristic of their hardworking nature. My father, upon arriving in the United States, went to college but also worked a variety of jobs. He was extremely frugal during the years as a college student in order to pay tuition as well as support his family back home; there was also the matter of learning English and adjusting to the American lifestyle. My mother faced similar obstacles and worked night shifts at the post office, while still making the time to care for my siblings and me. They started from such humble beginnings, lacking some of the qualities and abilities many would consider necessities for success. However, their struggle to speak fluent English showed their determination to continue walking the path they had chosen and to achieve their dreams.

Even as a young child, I understood the importance of doing well in school. It was something I learned from my parents—to choose a life I wanted to live and pursue it with an unfading conviction. I wanted to excel in academics, for it would make my parents proud and it would be beneficial to my prospective future. However, doing well in school was and has continued to be a challenge. My elementary school offered the Gifted and Talented Education (GATE) program to give gifted students a more challenging and satisfying education, and though my sister was admitted to the GATE program in first grade, I was not.

When I was in third grade, my parents, my brother, and my sister attended a GATE orientation at school. Although I was invited to go inside the classroom in which the orientation was held, I was not a GATE student. So I chose to stay outside, because I felt I was not accepted. However, while I waited outside, I knew that I wanted to be part of that meeting someday. I wanted to be a gifted student. My failure in being admitted to the program made the prospect of actually being admitted even more golden. By the end of that night, I made a choice to work diligently in spite of my abilities. The following year, I became a GATE student. Like my parents, I refused to accept the limitations of my abilities. I made the choice to work harder and achieve my goals in spite of any natural abilities I possessed.

When I think about choices and determination, I also think about legendary figures in history whom I've learned about over the years. Such figures were important people because they chose to stand up for what they believed in, despite being seemingly minute entities facing monumental issues. An iconic person who truly represents this ideal is Tank Man, the anonymous bystander who stood in front of advancing tanks in Beijing following the protests for democratic reform in Tiananmen Square in June 1989. There was a poster in one of my classes at school of Tank Man blocking the tanks. Every time I stared at the mysterious man in the poster, I felt an aura of passion and determination. The man clearly understood the grim consequences of his action as

a lone individual against an overpowering force, but he still chose to block the tanks from proceeding. His courageous act earned him international recognition as a symbol of freedom.

It is true that with choices made, feelings of regret may follow. However, if you—like Harry—have the chance to use a Pensieve, then look through my memories. You will find that the thing I regret the most is not any of my decisions, but the limitations of my own aspirations and imagination. Everyone has the power to choose a life that they want and strive to achieve it. I do not walk a trail filled with others' footsteps. Rather, I walk a path I have paved myself—a path that I have chosen.

Raymond graduated as one of his class salutatorians and an International Baccalaureate diploma recipient. He attends the University of California, Berkeley, where he is majoring in chemical biology. He is involved in UCB's Regents' and Chancellor's Scholars Association and is a co-coordinator of the Academic/Peer Advising Committee. He plays classical piano and has recently started to learn to play the ukulele.

A Piece of Fruit

by Andreea Tanase

I wonder how often people stop and consider life from someone else's perspective. For myself, I've noticed that not only do I overlook others' viewpoints, but I make little attempt to understand and imagine adopting another person's way of thinking and their way of life. Of course, it is impossible to completely grasp someone else's perception of life, but how many times does it even consciously cross our minds?

Too often, I forget that the server at a restaurant, the politician, the pastor, the janitor, and the nurse are much more than just their job titles. In this society, I am quick to label, categorize, and judge others without making the slightest attempt to understand who my fellow man is. In my interactions with people, I continue to overlook one basic fact again and again. Arguably, it is the most basic fact of all, and that is that I am a member of the human race. And because I am human and on my own quest for happiness, I find it a constant challenge to step outside myself and see what others are faced with in their lives. It has been so easy to become caught up solely in the matters of self-interest, and time and again, I fail to give equal value to others when they don't live the way I think they should.

I am beginning to see that how people treat one another is at the root of many problems plaguing society. For me, truly accepting others for everything they are is pivotal to living a life of happiness. This means that I must commit to living a life as free of ignorance as possible. Consequently, I must live my life awake and in acceptance of others. Although this may seem like a simple principle to live by, it is far from easy, and the transition from ignorance to enlightenment has been anything but smooth for me. In my own experience, the hardest part has been stopping myself from judging people based on just a single aspect about them, since there are countless other facts that I will never know about that make them unique.

In the past, when I saw a homeless man pushing his grocery cart full of a mismatched collection of junk, I used to wonder what mistakes he must have made to get himself in that situation. I would see a pregnant teenager and assume she must have had a chaotic upbringing or an undisciplined lifestyle. I would watch the news and see yet another politician caught in a scandal and think what a terrible person he must be, in all aspects of his life. Unfortunately, I have made all of these types of judgments, and I struggle with how easily they come for me. If I am to live my life connected, however, the most important step in changing the way I view others is being able to recognize when I make these judgments. I must realize that my disapproval is not acceptable and is often completely ignorant.

In Arthur Miller's play *Death of a Salesman,* as Willy Loman is getting fired, he tells his boss, "You can't eat the orange and throw the peel away—a man is not a piece of fruit!" Willy's declaration speaks volumes about the need for all of us to have compassion for others, no matter their circumstances, no matter their stature in life, no matter their place in or contribution to society. I have struggled with holding people up to what I think they should be, instead of looking at their journeys. It seems that our worth is not just in what we can give to society but in who we are as people. At times, I still forget that, but I'm trying to learn and see people differently. And I, for one, know that I would hate to be picked, peeled, eaten, and then just thrown away.

Andreea was born in Slatina, Romania, and immigrated to the United States with her parents when she was eight years old. She completed a two-year honors program at Riverside Community College and went on to attend the University of California, Los Angeles, where she plans to major in English. Andreea is an avid writer and is planning to pursue a career in the publishing industry. She enjoys being politically active and taking part in humanitarian work. She also loves living in Los Angeles and spends her weekends exploring Southern California in search of the meaning of life.

Common Sense Rounded Out

by Sebastian Chiu

When asked about my once-in-a-lifetime experience at the Summer Science Program in New Mexico this past summer, I'll enthusiastically start describing the six-week firestorm of problem sets, lectures, and asteroid tracking sessions. Usually, people respond with an amused but slightly hesitant chuckle. Occasionally, though, they'll ask, "So, what kind of science did you learn there?"

And I'll answer that, more than anything, I learned about what I affectionately call "true" science. Now, you might ask, "What do you mean by 'true' science?"

Allow me to explain: early one morning, several of us were just waking up and casually talking when the topic of superconductors came up, ravaging our sleep-deprived reverie. The single mention of superconductors provoked a heated argument about superconductor technology in all of its technical glory. And though I was the only one there without a prep-school education, countless science-fair victories, or any knowledge whatsoever about superconductors, I felt compelled to offer my two cents. I blurted out, "Isn't there more to it, though?"

Everyone stopped talking and flashed curious looks at me. "What do you mean?" someone asked. And without my realizing what I was going to say, out popped an experimental design of "true" science:

Title: Selecting an optimal rice-serving technique.

Introduction: It's a fact: as the rice server at church, I was once respected for my fiery speed and efficiency, but this all changed with a single realization. It struck me that just serving rice quickly was no longer sufficient to me.

Materials: Rice-serving equipment and 150 hungry mouths to feed each week.

Procedure: I started trying new serving techniques. I determined it would be a good change of pace and that I could potentially improve my technique in the process.

Observations: I'll be frank; most new styles struck me as outright dull. One particular method, however, did stand out. I tried putting rice on the plate, clutching the plate with both hands, turning to the recipient, and then courteously presenting the plate with a joyful, "Here you go!" Lo and behold, this method evoked an overwhelmingly heartwarming reception from church members.

Conclusion: This newly established method produced gratifying responses and garnered a more fulfilling outcome than purely using speed. Unfortunately, it got me nothing but trouble from our kitchen manager, who constantly yelled at me for being too slow. So I had to ask: "Where did I go wrong?"

By the end of my tale, amidst a shower of slaphappy laughs, superconductors had been completely driven out of the conversation. But honestly! It forced me to see something entirely new in my view of science. My summer experience wasn't significant because it centered on exploring technical math, physics, and astronomy topics, but because these explorations showed me the importance of "true" science. My rice-serving experiment actually enlightened me with an extraordinary realization. In fact, "true" science is ultimately learning with the understanding that what we choose to do with what we learn is a direct reflection of ourselves and the society we live in. "True" science is using experience and reason to uncover deeper truths beneath the facts.

And so, regardless of how simple or complicated it is, "true" science is the study of the physical world around us, which lies beyond the laboratory and guides our lives and our discovery. As George Santayana noted in his book *The Life of Reason*, "Science is nothing but developed perception, interpreted intent, common sense rounded out and minutely articulated." Thus my greatest goal in life is to nurture my "true" scientist at heart. I've learned, after all, that science means nothing in isolation. It is, rather, the connection we make with it and with others that changes the world.

Sebastian graduated from high school as a co-valedictorian and International Baccalaureate diploma recipient. He attends Harvard University, studying applied mathematics. In his free time, Sebastian enjoys spending time with his family and friends, reading, counting things, drawing patterns, and exercising. Sebastian is a big fan of the Los Angeles Dodgers baseball team and the Vancouver Canucks hockey team. In the future, Sebastian hopes to either enter academia or work in finance.

Be the Change

by Sameer Patel

I was raised in two different worlds. I went to sleep under the roof of my parents—conservative Asian Indians whose background valued respect, education, religion, and family. Yet I was becoming more and more influenced by those who valued a false sense of respect on the streets, bragging about the money in their pockets and women on their arms, spending late nights causing a ruckus, inhaling plants that caused pleasing sensations, and promoting violence. I was astounded at how easily I could fit into both lifestyles.

It was only after many mistakes and horrible experiences that I realized my generation had fallen prey to a plague. We are victims of brainwashing by incessant media and pop culture. Though all of us are born with good hearts, it is the experiences we face that shape us into who we are. We are told what defines beauty. We are told what is "cool." We are told what should be pleasing to us by the very people who, just coincidentally, create the products that can make us into exactly who they tell us we are supposed to be.

In high school, I was respected for my lyrical ability, and music started to become more than a hobby, more than a way to express what I saw and how I felt. Music became my tool to earn respect wherever I went. Again, popular music is something on which society has placed value, but I didn't see the danger in this. Musicians are revered more than scientists; one who entertains is worth more than one who saves lives. Using excessive profanity, portraying women in a derogatory way, and praising money over all other things, I was the typical hip-hop artist rapping the typical lyrics about the typical lifestyle that most of these "gangsters" never truly lived to begin with. I knew this because it was far from the truth for me as well, even as I sang the words that brought me notoriety. How were we to know that we were merely products of a corporate music industry that fed off suburban kids' fantasies by giving them music portraying a lifestyle of no worries and no limits? After all, there are few who *aren't* intrigued by that lifestyle, at least on some level.

Only when I started spending time with new friends did I snap out of my little fantasy and realize what I had really become. I had involved myself with a group of people who had all the wrong morals but somehow justified their behavior and made themselves think what they were doing was right. Who was I to speak badly of them? After all, I had fallen for it, too. But there's a part of me that still feels the shame of having been duped by false idols.

After this epiphany, well, that's when the lyrics changed, the mindset changed, and, most importantly, my outlook on the world changed. We live in a society in which we are so easily influenced by those around us. What would happen if we all had the right influences from the beginning? It occurred to me that we could all become each other's influence and inspiration. A few years ago, I was reading *A Walk in My Shoes* by Andrew Young, an American civil rights activist, and his godson, Kabir Sehgal. In this book, I read that Mahatma Gandhi once said you must "be the change you want to see in the world." I am inspired, daily, by his words, and I have let go of the dark influence of my past. I'm certain that we can each make a difference by trying to be exactly how we want others to be, or at least by working toward this goal.

My music has become how I achieve this. My lyrics have become about changes that I wish to see in myself and in our world. My friends and the people around me see that I am trying my hardest to make these changes. If the song I sing is about spreading peace and being open to people of all faiths and colors, I make sure I am doing just that and encouraging all my friends to do the same. I know, though, that the best way to influence is to be an example. The best way to show others is by doing so myself. I know today that I must be an agent of change, and that gives me all the hope in the world for our future.

Sameer attends the College of Dental Medicine at Western University of Health Sciences. Along with pursuing a career in dentistry, Sameer is heavily involved in the Los Angeles music scene. In 2009, he released his own album, The Makings of Mr. Patel, *which has sold over 1,000 copies. Sameer is also involved in a wide range of humanitarian work, including tutoring high school students and volunteering at medical clinics.*

God Himself

by Thomas Assali

As a little kid, I grew up feeling comfortable using the phrase "It's not fair!" As children grow up, whenever they do not get what they want, frequently they will say "But that's not fair!" And indeed, many people realize that this phrase is overused. As a child, however, I didn't just use it. No, I *lived* that phrase as though there were no tomorrow. In fact, I continued to develop through my years clinging to that motto as a way of life. Today, it has become a major influence on my morals, beliefs, and actions. Fairness has become beautifully integrated with my internal system of rules. I have become so attached to this concept that in simple decisions, like talking to friends, I will pursue "fairness" by talking to each friend an equal amount. One can only imagine, then, how important fairness is to me.

But, unfortunately, I find this world plagued with unfairness, and as driven as I have been to correct it, much of it is beyond my control. Time has shown me that our patience and tolerance for one another has been slowly diminishing, despite desegregation and other progress against racism. Events such as the tragedy of 9/11 created new tensions and a new group of people to hate. After 9/11, I felt ashamed to admit my heritage, a heritage of which I had always been so proud. I hated the terrorists as much as anyone—maybe more, in fact, for tainting my religion and culture with their extremist and hateful beliefs and actions.

Around this time, a friend of mine from middle school stopped talking to me after I told him the background of my family, even though we had been friends for years. Fear had unfairly changed his opinion of me, and though nothing in my religion condones the violence used by the terrorists, fear still won over. Fear has made people become, again, less tolerant of others, and it only seems to be getting worse.

Often the consequences of unfairness are subtle, almost minuscule, depending on the situation. I worry most when I see it even among college students, who are allegedly beyond this kind of prejudice because they are "educated." I see around me a strong lack of understanding for one another. Insults against African Americans, negative stereotypes about immigrants, terrorist accusations against Middle Easterners, and Christian-bashing are just a few examples of this intolerance. As an advocate of fairness, it upsets me that I have to live in a world with this kind of behavior.

In his book *How to Win Friends and Influence People*, Dale Carnegie, a successful professor in human relations, proposed what I believe to be the best solution for the global dilemma of unfairness. In this book, Carnegie states that condemning one another invokes hatred and anger. Carnegie wrote that Samuel Johnson said, "God himself, sir, does not propose to judge man until the end of his days." This realization was truly marvelous. It has led me to a new application of fairness among people. If people didn't condemn or criticize each other, then many feelings of hatred and anger could be avoided, and there certainly has been nothing to suggest that treating one another unfairly can create any holistic benefit for our society. This kind of behavior actually limits the true potential of the human race, a race that has made so many remarkable, fascinating, and intriguing leaps in technology, medicine, and communication.

Desegregation was a huge step forward for tolerance, but there is still plenty of room for growth in today's society. It sometimes seems disheartening that the world's population is increasing, and the crowding of people coupled with the lightning-fast communication brought by technology often escalates the problem of intolerance.

I see how humanity needs to work harder to revive its ability to tolerate and accommodate the many differences we all have. There has never been a better time to do so, as global unrest continues and digital communication facilitates dissension between people. Mankind only shows its ignorance by allowing this kind of treatment to occur, and while some people will attempt to cover this up by justifying it as simply "human nature," it is also within human nature to seek happiness. That cannot be achieved if we cannot find peace with one another.

Moreover, I must keep my eyes set on nobler objectives, concerning myself with the progression of the human race as a whole. In my quest for "fairness," it is clear that I cannot fall victim to the ignorant and potentially dangerous temptation to treat others unfairly just because I have been maligned. I strongly believe that this change must begin at

the most personal level, and that is with my own thoughts and behavior. Today, I am committed to holding myself to an even higher standard of fairness and becoming a role model for those who are still tempted to judge others. After all, if God doesn't judge, then—as Carnegie writes—"why should you and I?"

Thomas attends the University of California, Irvine. He plans to pursue a career in clinical medicine. When he's not studying, Thomas enjoys traveling, tasting new foods, and exploring different cultures. He also likes to work out and maintain a healthy physique.

A Hot Bath

by Emili Lamph

Hitting the snooze button for an extra five minutes of sleep, or the way your heart goes into overdrive and your vocal cords fail you when you see the one you adore. Putting your favorite song on repeat, and knowing every single line of that song by heart. Finding money in your pocket. The changing of the seasons. Remembering the name of that actor that a few moments ago you couldn't put your finger on, and gold stars in elementary school. These are just a few of the little things that I swear by. Sylvia Plath's protagonist in *The Bell Jar* states that there "must be quite a few things a hot bath won't cure, but I don't know many of them." She compares a hot bath to a cure-all. Similarly, I find that the small things, maybe even the ones I overlook at times, are the details in life that make it special, a life worth treasuring. It's the little things that make a difference to me. It's the little things that make life worth living.

Often people say that when encountering a near-death experience, their life flashes before their eyes, and I believe them. Maybe it's like a video watched in rewind, as if to remind us of all the wonderful things life has given—the little things that we dismiss on a daily basis until they're taken away. I have complete faith in the moment, or, actually, in a mosaic of little moments that make up the sum total of a life. My first kiss, playing in the park with my big sister, Christmas and all of its beauty, laughing and crying with my best friends, watching a beach sunset, and sweet dreams might be the portrait of my life, of how happiness would be reflected if it flashed in front of my eyes if I were suddenly to leave this world. And in these moments, calmness and joy would be captured and wrapped up in a box of little things.

One may argue that big events are the ones that people use to evaluate a life. After all, even Plath was unable to take her own advice. She couldn't bridge the gap between the painful disappointments in life and life's myriad little pieces of happiness. Yet it's the little things that get us to those big events. A wedding would not be possible without a first date, learning each other's quirks, and saying "I love you" for the first time. If you think about it, on our way to achieving those big goals we set for ourselves, it's the little things that bring us all genuine joy.

These specks of bliss keep me going so often. Conversing with people through quotes from favorite movies. Listening to oldies all day long. Iced tea. Inside jokes. Crying at the end of *Titanic,* regardless of how many times I've watched it before. Using song titles by the Beatles to describe the way I feel at any given moment. Walking into my best friend's home as if it were my own. Painting my nails to reflect my mood. Running into an old friend. Chocolate of any kind. Commercial-free television.

Spontaneously driving to the beach in the summer. Making others smile. Smiling myself. Eating Thanksgiving dinner, even in April or August. Singing along while watching *The Sound of Music*. Cookies with cold milk. Standing and looking up into falling snow or settling in at home just before it rains. The scent of citrus in summer and the taste of cinnamon in winter. It's the little things that cure whatever's ailing me.

Born and raised in Southern California, Emili attends the University of California, Riverside. Emili plans to declare her major as English. She is a lover of the beach, faith, the Beatles, soccer, celebrity heartthrobs, and the company of her friends and family.

It Lights the Way

by Koutaiba Chihabi

Though high school is not long behind me, it seems so far away. If you knew me then and spoke with me now, you would know that I am no longer the person I used to be. While my personality has remained fairly similar, and my opinions on political issues have remained fairly consistent, I am spiritually a different being. I now see life through a different perspective, and it has opened up so many doors for me.

You see, I was born a Muslim. At the word, many images have probably already popped up in your head. You don't need to tell me what images you see, but I am certain they do not represent what Islam truly stands for, and even I was ignorant about some aspects of my own religion not so long ago.

My first year in college, some of my peers were taking a comparative religions class, which thoroughly studied the world's three Abrahamic religions: Judaism, Christianity, and Islam. At the time, I was a somewhat practicing Muslim but I didn't follow all of the teachings. It's not because

I didn't believe them, but more because I didn't see the necessity, nor did I have the desire to pray five times a day. I always turned to God when I was in need, but never to simply give thanks for being alive. The irony of this is that the Qur'an ponders this very aspect of humankind. It constantly reminds man that he prays for help and guidance when he suffers, but when God grants him mercy, he once again turns his back on God until he is in need again.

As I continued to spend more time with these friends who took the comparative religions course, I became more interested in my own beliefs. I questioned why I was Muslim if I have read neither the Qur'an nor the Bible, and so I did just that. I bought a Bible and an English Qur'an and I spent a month reading both. And yes . . . my grades did suffer, but to me it was worth every second. I then proceeded to spend countless hours at the library and borrowed an average of eight books a week on the history of religion—everything from ancient Judaism to Christianity and modern Islam. I read and read and read.

It was the historical evidence that changed my views and confirmed my faith in Islam. It became clear to me that Islam's core message was—and continues to be—that all the prophets, from Adam to Abraham, from Moses to Noah to Jesus, and all the way to Muhammad (Peace be upon them all), have come from God. In fact, they all taught the same message, which was to worship One God.

After all this researching, I came to realize that this journey of prophets makes sense, as supported through their own scriptures. It all finally came together in my mind. It has been from this point onward that I began my new life as what I consider to be a true Muslim. What many people do not know is that the word *Muslim* in Arabic means "One who submits his or her desires to God," and *Islam* means "Submission to God." This is where I consider myself to have become a Muslim, not from birth, but from understanding.

My seeking of knowledge and reading did not end there, however. It turns out that this intense craving to learn and seek is a core belief of my religion as well. The Qur'an commands Muslims to acquire knowledge, for those who are of knowledge are not comparable to those without it. This idea is furthered by the Islamic prophet, who commands, "Acquire knowledge: it enables its possessor to distinguish right from the wrong, it lights the way to heaven . . . it guides us to happiness; it sustains us in misery; it is an ornament among friends and an armor against enemies."

And it is this message that guides every bit of my life. Through knowledge, I become closer to God. My pursuit of science before my spiritual journey was simply because it fascinated me. Now, my pursuit of knowledge is because it brings me closer to God. I feel that by learning about the ingenuity of His creation, by learning about the perfection in the laws of nature, I feel closer to Him.

I now lead my life with this deep conviction of pursuing knowledge. I no longer see studying as laborious, but rather enjoyable. I see my education as more valuable than simply a degree. Instead, it is a key to unlocking the secrets of our world. Wherever I go, whatever I do, I do it to seek closeness to God. For how can we truly know God if we don't seek to know His creation?

Koutaiba was born in Syria, and moved to Riverside, California, with his family when he was five. He attends the University of California, Los Angeles, where he is a neuroscience major. He plans to continue his studies at UCLA, pursuing a Ph.D. in neuroscience, as well as furthering his Islamic studies. He led a successful campaign to prevent the closure of UCLA's Islamic studies program, and he is helping research the genetic basis for bipolar disorder.

Man's First Duty

by James Roose

At times, I can be rather focused on myself as an individual. It seems, therefore, that I would easily align with an author such as Ayn Rand. She espouses a philosophy called Objectivism, which promotes individualism and creativity while condemning collective action and altruistic notions. This philosophy is outlined by Howard Roark, the protagonist of Rand's novel *The Fountainhead*. Roark emphatically proclaims that the "first right on earth is the right of the ego. Man's first duty is to himself." Ironically, I still identify with this statement, not because of my past blind agreement with its message, but because of my present vehement disagreement with Rand's sentiment. This polar reversal of my own philosophy stems from reading Rand's novel while participating in Science Smart, an activity that changed my philosophy toward poverty and its effect on children.

Science Smart is an activity in which high school students travel to local childcare centers to teach children about basic science and its importance to society. El Centro de Niños, one of the centers I visited, was not much more than a rundown shack. It lacked air conditioning, the carpets were old and dirty, and the paint was peeling from the walls. I quickly realized that the children there would go to schools like mine, schools that enrolled many students from families who lived near or below the poverty level.

Unfortunately, I had previously failed to realize the impact of these disadvantaged students' home situations on their academics and choices. Until reading Rand's novel and participating in Science Smart, I had mistakenly believed that many students simply did not want to learn and had turned to drugs or alcohol because of a lack of self-control. The experience of observing the children at El Centro de Niños truly changed my perspective on this issue. I was leaning toward Rand's philosophy and embracing my own "right of the ego" before Science Smart, but as I talked to small groups of children about the sun and dinosaurs, I was reminded that they were not bad people who somehow lacked ability or moral fiber, as Rand's ideology suggests. Also, poor decisions that may lead them to future drug abuse or gang violence are not just the result of societal flaws, such as an absence of jobs, lack of parental guidance, and a poorly funded education system. The future of all these children is affected by people's individualized responses to circumstances, as well as by possible socioeconomic challenges.

Now, when I step back and examine the world these children come from, I realize that their negative path in life is neither one of their own making nor one that they deserve. In this case, Rand's philosophy simply cannot apply. A child's "right of the ego" will not create jobs or end peer pressure, nor will it create a supportive family where one did not exist before. My "right of the ego" will not do these things for that child, and a stranger's "right of the ego" will not do it either. For this reason, society must make a concerted effort to end or at least reduce the cyclical poverty that condemns so many young people to unproductive—and, in unfortunate cases, short—lives. In this case, collective action is necessary, and in direct contradiction to Rand, I propose that sometimes man must put aside his "right of the ego" and make it his first duty to help others. Then, beyond being willing to help others, I hope to allow myself to engage in more balanced and equal relationships in which I care as much about someone else as they care about me. I believe that I have a duty to make myself happy. But my own happiness surely depends on how I treat those close to me, and this is part of man's duty as well.

James graduated as a co-valedictorian of his high school class and is studying computational biology at Brown University. He plans to attend graduate school before working in medical or pharmaceutical research. James enjoys playing soccer and spending time with his friends. James is known for being quiet in large groups yet overly frank in more intimate conversation.

All We Have to Decide

by Gregory Hice

In my life, I have read many books. I have read countless pages of defined as well as undefined wisdom. Therefore, it is extremely difficult to come up with only one defining quote for my life. I'd have to admit, though, that one stands out and reflects my own ideology beyond all others. In J.R.R. Tolkien's *The Fellowship of the Ring,* the first book in the Lord of the Rings trilogy, the character Frodo learns that there is going to be a great battle in his lifetime. Frodo tells Gandalf that he wishes it didn't have to happen while he was alive. Gandalf replies, "So do I . . . and so do all who live to see such times. But that is not for them to decide. All we have to decide is what to do with the time that is given us." These are words that I now live by. Gandalf is referring to the fact that Frodo, like others, might have to make difficult choices for the greater good of the world. This is applicable not only to me, but to everyone in the world, and I see how this could benefit all of us in these unsettling times.

This is a dark but also inspiring way to approach a bleak epoch of any troubled society, which is why I like what Gandalf says and feel so strongly connected to his message. The dedication we must have to find a way to live our lives, despite the hard times we live in, inspires me. All around us, we see countless people losing their jobs and their homes. Our country has been part of a war lasting longer than World War II, and the economy is at its lowest since the Great Depression. Though our era is not to be confused with other periods in history when humankind also struggled and seemed lost and in great despair, we are clearly in a state of modern crisis.

In spite of these hardships, I, along with everyone else, still manage to do good things. Despite all that is bad, I am inspired when I see others lending a hand, reaching out to their fellow man. We do everything from building homes for the homeless to donating food to those who don't have anything to eat. We send clothes and shoes and blankets to help people we have never met and know we will never see face-to-face. Through myriad other acts of kindness, I see good all around me. This is one of the things that I have taken from Tolkien's writing. I think he wanted us to make use of our time and find a way to do good things for others, no matter what our circumstances are and what is happening in the world around us.

This is ultimately why I live by these words and why his sentiment is something that *everyone* can learn to live by. For those of us who have something extra to share, we have to use what we have wisely, to help those who feel they have nothing. For those who have lost their way and claim they have nothing to give, we can help them until they can stand up for themselves. When we help each other, even in the smallest of ways, we are making use of our time. We can inspire people so that others can decide to make use of their time as well.

We all have a limited number of days in this world, and we have to make the most of them and help others, especially in times such as these. I know that I will continue to do what I can to help those in need and work daily on thinking beyond my own desires. I also know that it is not for me to decide how others live their lives or how they spend their time. But it *is* up to me to decide how I live mine, so I will be an example for my peers and hope that I can help with these great challenges that we are facing. I will make the most of my time here while I can, with the time that has been given to me. That is what I have decided.

Gregory attends the University of Riverside as an electrical engineering major. He enjoys all manner of creativity, from writing stories to composing music to designing video games. Those activities, along with experiencing others' creativity, are what he does in his free time.

And So...

Questions for Reflection, Discussion, and Writing

Throughout your life, you have been exposed to the beliefs and ideals of your family, friends, community, and other groups. As you've grown up, making leaps and bounds in your physical, mental, and emotional development, maybe you've also heard a small voice inside of you asking, "But what do *you* think?"

And so . . . what *do* you think? What do you believe, and what do you value?

Sometimes, your ideals probably match those of others. Other times, you may want to forge your own path. And still other times, you might not be sure. Figuring out the answers to these big questions is something everyone has to do on his or her own. The following questions may get you thinking about beliefs and ideals, themes explored in this part's essays.

Karisa notes her lack of motivation to follow through with a reading assignment because it required extra effort to complete. However, when she goes back and reads the assigned book, she sees that the effort was worthwhile. Have you ever taken a shortcut to get around work at school, at home, or elsewhere—or been tempted to? How did that experience turn out? What are the pros and cons of taking shortcuts? Do you think that sometimes shortcuts are justified? Why or why not?

Raymond reflects on the importance of making careful, conscious choices and sticking to our beliefs. In his case, he devotes himself to pursuing his education. What beliefs do you choose to stand up for or pursue? How did this belief come to mean so much to you, and what would you be willing to do to defend it?

Andreea recognizes her own tendency to judge others based on their external qualities and circumstances. Do you find yourself making similar judgments about others? If so, how might you shift your focus to valuing the inner core of a person? If you could decide what criteria others used to judge *you*, what would you choose?

Sebastian shares his revelation about science, learning, and knowledge, and their connections to the world as a whole. What do you think the purpose of learning is? How do you think knowledge should be used in the world?

Sameer suggests that he is responsible for making the changes in the world that he sees as necessary. What is a specific change that you'd like to make in your own, immediate world? What kinds of changes would you like to see in the bigger, broader world? Do these changes seem attainable? Overwhelming? How could you personally begin putting them into action?

Thomas alludes to the biases many of us feel, especially when we're afraid. Think about a bias that you might have toward a group of people. Try to confront your thoughts and fears honestly. Where do your feelings stem from? Have you ever met someone who was able to dispel some of your bias? How? Have *you* ever been the subject of this type of bias? If so, how did that feel? If not, imagine what that would be like.

Emili explores the simple things in life that she finds enjoyable, the things that make each day just a little brighter for her. List as many things as you can that you love. Try not to evaluate whether they're worthwhile or not. Just write or talk openly about the things that make your world nicer, no matter how small or significant they might be. Then, think about *why* these things bring you joy. Is there always a specific reason?

Koutaiba discusses his exploration of religion and spirituality, which are very personal aspects of being human. What are your beliefs about the existence of a higher power? What role, if any, does religion play in your life? Reflect on how your beliefs have developed. Are they from your upbringing? From education? From experiences you've had? Consider the differences and similarities between religion and spirituality and what each means to you.

James admits how easy it is to get caught up in our own agendas, and he shares his belief that a wholly self-centered life is empty. Write about an experience you've had when you were able to help someone else. How did you feel while you were helping him or her? Do you know how the other person felt after your help? What are your views about your duty or responsibility to others in this world?

Gregory addresses the importance of how he chooses to use his time. How do you use your time, whether at school, at home, or elsewhere? Do you think you're making the best use of your time, or would you like to make changes? How do you balance work and play in your life?

Part 2

Essays on Family, Friends, and Love

"S'pose you didn't have nobody."
—Crooks in John Steinbeck's *Of Mice and Men*

Miles to Go

by Anthony Accuar

Before I was even born, an event took place that would shape the way I lived. On May 5, 1990, my older brother was involved in a fatal car crash. He was only 16 years old and, until that moment, seemed to have a long life in front of him. My parents suffered a great loss, and I have made it a point not to make them ever suffer again. Throughout my life, I have pushed myself to thrive in school. Not only have I pushed myself academically, but I am as honest and helpful to my parents as possible. Tomorrow isn't promised to anyone, and if I were to die, I would want people to reflect on my life and see that I was a good person and lived my life to the fullest. Often, I wonder, "What if?" But I try not to live with any regrets. Because of my knowledge about how short and how precious life is, I try to do as much as possible with the time I have been given.

At the beginning of my sophomore year in high school, I started to take online classes at the community college with the goal of graduating from college before I graduated from high school. I knew that my parents expected me to do well in school and put my best effort toward anything, but I also think my drive to succeed came from being so painfully aware that I may not have had the chance to do it the next day. When it was one o'clock in the morning and I was still doing my high school homework, when I was so tired that I just wanted to put my head down and sleep for the next week, I thought of my brother and how he didn't have the chance to live out his life. In a way, I did (and still do) things for my brother to show that I am living life, a life that he never had the chance to finish.

Not long ago, I found myself walking down a grassy field, obtaining my associate's degree, and two weeks after that I was walking down another field, receiving my high school diploma. Looking to the sky, I kept thinking to myself how proud my brother would be of me. I had accomplished something very few students have done, and although this was a great feeling, I started to feel tired, so tired. Because I'd done so much in such a short amount of time, I started to think that I deserved to take a break.

And I guess I do take breaks. I spend time with my friends, talk on the phone, chat online, and help my mom with her business. I try to take all the small things in life in stride and not think too much about the mistakes I have made, because what happened yesterday cannot be changed today. My brother didn't wear a seatbelt, and because of this one small mistake, he's no longer with us. We all would like to go back and change that, but we can't. We have to live with what's been done and with what can't be undone.

But it seems that, more and more, I have this internal struggle pulling me in separate directions. Even though I want to believe that I have plenty of time and my whole life before me, I keep thinking that life could be over in an instant and I have to make the most of it. I was born into painful circumstances. With my brother's life cut short and my parents' great loss, it was a difficult life for a young boy to step into. But as the poet Robert Frost wrote in "Stopping by Woods on a Snowy Evening," "I have promises to keep / And miles to go before I sleep." I feel I must find a way to keep a self-made promise, this commitment to live my life to the fullest. More and more often these days, I want to slow down just a little and enjoy life as it comes. Maybe living life to the fullest means knowing how short and precious life is and making the best of my days because tomorrow is so uncertain. I just don't want to live it all so fast and cram so much into life that I entirely miss the point. And here's what I think the point is:

I truly admire what a good person my brother was and how he was able to be a light to all of his friends even well beyond his death. He has been a light to me, and as I walk the many miles to my next destination, I hope I can find a balance. I hope I can find the balance to value every minute as if it were my last, but also to live with the expectation that I have the time I need to find my way and become a light for others who will follow in my footsteps.

Anthony plans to transfer from the University of California, Riverside, to the University of Southern California, where he will major in business. He is working on setting up a website to make books and other supplies more affordable for University of California students, and he also helps his mom run a local popcorn company. In the future, he hopes to work with stocks and bonds.

By Any Other Name

by Jessica Trumble

I am the furthest thing from a romantic. All that Romeo and Juliet nonsense? I'm far too practical for that. Those teenage girls who "fall in love" every week utterly appall me. That's not to say I don't believe in love at all; I just don't believe in teenage love. By the way, I'm also a complete hypocrite.

I was never going to fall in love as a teenager. That was one of the only things of which I'd ever been truly certain. Love was something I couldn't even define, so I certainly wasn't about to dive into it head over heels. That's why no one was surprised when I was the picture of maturity while dating my first boyfriend. We met in the ninth grade, and began dating as sophomores. During our two years together, I never once strayed from my antagonistic stance toward teenage love. That all changed after we broke up.

After things went south with the boyfriend, as these things often do, it felt more like a divorce than anything else. Who would get our mutual friends? Our lunch spot?

I struggled to find a balance, leaning on my friends for support while trying not to smother them with my own selfish concerns. It was through this process of relying on my closest friends that I discovered the love I had so venomously disapproved of before. He had been an acquaintance who turned into a close friend, and he had become my rock during another, earlier difficult time in my life. And I fell in love with him.

I really never planned it. The feelings seemed to seep through my body, like a warm drink on a cold day. They were completely unforeseen and just as shocking for me as they were for those who knew me well.

I know I'm horrifying both of our families by sharing this information, but it's the truth. Being in love didn't inspire me to start spewing lollipops and rainbows, and the thought of wedding bells and baby names offends me to this day. Though our relationship has since ended, the effect it had on my opinion of teenage love has not. The love we had was crazy and surprising and wonderful, and I am grateful to have experienced it. It changed me, and I believe that change was for the better. Having a little more faith in love and the good things in life is something everyone could use.

I recognize that a major influence on my distrust of teenage love is the way adults discuss the relationships of those younger than them, with condescension emanating from their every word. The truth is, your first love is just as painful as it is wonderful. Unless you marry your high school sweetheart, chances are you're going to get your heart broken, and it's going to hurt. But by belittling the importance of young love, adults diminish the value of this experience and dismiss these emotions. They tell themselves that the love between two inexperienced teens is nothing but silly school yard nonsense. And yet, as Shakespeare ponders in *Romeo and Juliet,* "What's in a name? That which

we call a rose / By any other name would smell as sweet."
Love, on any terms, at any age and by whatever name you
want to call it, is still love. Maybe by denying this—by
dismissing it as "puppy love"—we can convince ourselves
that our own experiences were not as painful as they
seemed. And maybe this is the only way we find the courage
to love again.

Even having been in love, I'm still my pragmatic self.
I have grown to recognize the difference between allowing life to surprise me and letting my true self become
distorted as I adjust to fit into my world. I still believe in
putting studying before dating, putting my family before
my friends, and saying good-night in a timely fashion.
Nonetheless, I am now a believer. Maybe I'm being just as
silly as everyone else; maybe I have become the thing I can't
stand. Or maybe love is more universal than I once had the
ability to accept as true. And maybe, just maybe, Romeo and
Juliet weren't nonsense after all.

*Jessica attends the University of California, Los Angeles, and has
absolutely no idea what she wants to do with her life. She is a member
of the On-Campus Housing Council and is active in the university's
student government. She was also one of two student editors of this
book. In Jessica's free time, she enjoys watching reruns of* Friends *with
friends.*

So Little

by Asma Patel

I've heard many of my friends say in passing that they can't
wait to graduate and leave this place and all these people
behind. They act like they never want to see anyone from
high school again, and I can't help but wonder why. The
amount of faith that we put into the longevity of our friendships after high school seems ridiculously low. We spend
four years creating relationships that apparently are supposed to last only while we are in high school. We seem to
use these relationships merely as a means of getting by in
high school, and we have so little trust in each other. It's
odd that we keep the lifelong lessons that we learn in high
school longer than those who have helped us learn them.

Imagine high school all over again if we were to stay
true to ourselves, if we trusted one another with the real
us. Too bad it won't ever happen, at least for me. My four
years of observing my friends as they loved and fought were

four years of fabricated tears and meaningless hugs. My high school experience has definitely been defined by some good times, but mostly by aggravating attitudes and endless quibbles. When I think back on many of my experiences, I laugh at the foolish situations in which I was placed. I question how two people who hated each other one day could all of a sudden be best friends two weeks later. I reflect on the way true colors seem to shine through the nearer we all get to turning our tassels and moving on.

Coming into high school, I wanted everyone to like me. So, of course, I decided that the *last* thing I should do was act like my real self. Ironically, I saw that I was able to trust the ones who were further from me more than those whom I considered my best friends. I wasn't able to confide in those with whom I spent the most time, those people who appeared closest to me. Over the years, I met people who showed me their inner selves and others who hid behind facades. I started to realize the emptiness in pretending to be someone I wasn't, and that there was little point in trusting only those whom I held at bay. The truth is, I know I won't be able to hide the real me forever. By assuming these personalities and attitudes, all of us at some point are bound to burst. Maybe that's why, in this last year of high school, I have seen best friends become enemies and enemies become role models. I must admit, I have learned from them all.

As I began to come out with my true self, I was able to accomplish so much more. I earned greater respect from people when I revealed my true feelings and I was able to get along better with the people I once treated as my enemies. How different everything would be if we had just shared these truths about ourselves when we all first met.

Not only would we spend less time trying to impress people we might never really get close to, but we would learn to trust our own judgment of the character of others, and we would surround ourselves with people who really deserve our friendship.

A wise young girl, Anne Frank, who didn't have the benefit of seeing her graduation day, noted in *The Diary of a Young Girl*, "Why do we trust one another so little? I know there must be a reason, but still I sometimes think it's horrible that you can never really confide in people, even in those who are nearest to you." I haven't had much chance to reflect back on what high school has meant to me overall, but I want to start college with fresh eyes, an open heart, and a willingness to trust others, so I can skip the drama and get right to the good stuff.

Asma attends the University of the Pacific, where she's in a six-year dental program and is getting her biological sciences degree. At UOP, Asma has started the "Swipes Against Hunger and Violence" project, which in its first year raised over $8,000 for a homeless shelter. Her interest in fund-raising and community service goes back to high school, where she helped organize a Haiti Relief Concert for the Red Cross Club, raising more than $1,500 in one hour.

See It Through

by Rachele Honcharik

My opinions and beliefs are ever-changing, and different experiences tend to lead me in directions I never imagined I would take. There are many choices, big and small, that I make every day and that make me question who I think I am or who I want to be. I have a really difficult time defining myself and expressing a personal philosophy, because I feel like I am constantly growing and changing. There is one idea that I have stayed true to, though, and that's to go after something I want even if I know the odds are against me. I think this comes from my desire to experience everything life has to offer and to learn something from each decision and outcome. Moreover, it's from watching my mom and the way she has lived her life.

If there is one trait I have taken from my mother, it is her courage. In *To Kill a Mockingbird*, the protagonist's father, Atticus Finch, defines courage as knowing "you're licked before you begin but you begin anyways and you see it through no matter what. You rarely win, but sometimes you do." Like most mothers, my mom wants the best for me. She encourages me to seize every opportunity and use it to its fullest potential. She has encouraged me to reach for those opportunities that may even seem impossible. After all, she does this every day.

When friends meet my mom for the first time they are often taken aback, and when they get me alone for a second, they scold me for not telling them my mom is in a wheelchair. It shocks them, and initially they don't want this emotion to show on their faces when they shake her hand and say hello.

In my defense, I never think to mention that my mom is in a wheelchair. When she was just 14 years old, she fell off a ladder and broke her back. It was one of those freak accidents you never imagine could happen. She has been paralyzed from the waist down for most of her life, and all of mine. To me, though, she is just a regular mom. Like many of my friends' moms, she has always been there for me. When there were those moments as a child when I just needed to be held, I knew I could crawl onto my mother's lap and find comfort in her safe arms. When I needed a cheerleader on the sideline of my soccer games, she was always there. Mother, friend, confidante, teacher, nutrition-ist, chef, caregiver, banker, coach, consultant, and advisor—my mom has always been there for me. And when it was time to move out of the house, she was there helping me pack, hoping that everything I had learned from home would carry over into the next phase of my life. Like I said, just a regular, great mom.

On family vacations, my mother never sits out on an activity. Whether it means long arguments with hotel owners to create handicap accessible ramps or strapping herself to some stranger's lap in order to zip-line over the mountains of Costa Rica, we're all right there, helping her be a part of everything. Of course, there are some things that she can't do. She couldn't hike the volcano in Hawaii with the rest of the family or go cliff-jumping in Mexico or travel to Haiti to do relief work after the earthquake when my dad and sister and I flew over. But she always tries. She goes as far as she can. No matter how good or bad the chances are of something working out in her favor, she always tries.

From her life, I've seen that it takes a lot of courage to try as hard as she does, knowing that many times she will fail. Just as my mom faces challenges, I now face my challenges head-on with the same fervor. There is no sense in crying over a loss or failure if I know I gave it my best shot and made the most of the outcome. I won't have a single regret and I won't have to change a single thing, because I know that everything I've done has made me who I am and who I will become. I have learned from watching my mom that if I don't have the courage to try, even if the chances of failure are great, I will also never succeed. My choices are infinite, and not just because of the opportunities I've had. They are without bounds because my mother showed me how to live outside of limits.

Rachele attends the University of Southern California, studying broadcast and digital journalism with a minor in performing arts. She took one semester off to go to Kenya, where she worked with International Peace Initiatives. This organization provides homes for orphans and vulnerable children, supports grassroots organizations and community leaders, and provides training in peace education and conflict resolution.

Most of the Time

by Saad Patel

What does a recovering addict and rock star have in common with me, a college-bound high school senior? The answer is simple: perspective. Anthony Kiedis, the lead singer of Red Hot Chili Peppers, has lived an unimaginably difficult life, complete with abandonment, drug addictions, and near-death experiences. In terms of life events, mine are in no distinguishable way related to his. Nevertheless, Kiedis's approach to life perfectly captures the perspective that has inspired the way I approach mine. Kiedis is the type of person to pursue challenges and try to accomplish them individually, while at the same time understanding that asking for help is more than acceptable. As he said in his autobiography, "I'd rather have a challenge or even failure than something that was too freely given. Most of the time."

Likewise, I've often found myself seeking challenges over easy tasks. While this has motivated me to succeed in life, it wasn't until I came across Anthony's words that I understood the significance of "most of the time" and the importance of seeking advice and sometimes stepping out of my comfort zone.

When I was a child, my life was driven by competition, whether it was in school, sports, or even the Monopoly board game I played with my family. The satisfaction I received from doing well in my activities shaped my personality, for better or worse. Most of my competition was colored by my cousins, for they were my role models and I wanted to be just like them. Each summer, I abandoned soccer and schoolwork to spend my time with my favorite cousin, Shafique, who was very athletic and well read. I struggled to turn the pages of a novel as quickly as he did. I ignored the cramp in my stomach as I desperately fought to keep up with him on a bike. At the end of the day, my ambition to be the best failed, yet my determination was never lost. Little did I know then that each time I lost to Shafique, I was being humbled—I was learning the importance of humility that had seemingly been nonexistent in the men of my family.

The transition from elementary school to middle school coincided with Shafique's negative transformation due to the death of his father. Shafique's depression swallowed him into drug addiction and he distanced himself from my family almost completely. Thus, our bond was diminished, and as I reflect upon the past few years, I can clearly see the effect this has had on me. I immersed myself in my hobbies of playing soccer and skateboarding for hours on end. I applied the same approach toward my schoolwork and my arrogance developed, unchecked. I didn't realize that my callous personality was becoming a severe character flaw. I simply accepted my family's justification of my behavior as teenage angst. Although this may have been a factor, what other people didn't know and what I am certain of now is that I was secretly enraged by the sudden absence of Shafique from my life. He had been my role model, my shining star, and he was gone.

My perspective of life was altered, and as Anthony Kiedis immersed himself in music, I immersed myself in books. By the time I entered high school I had developed a full-blown love for literature. Reading had become my escape by the time I entered North High School, the only school that had the academic program of my parents' choosing. I was forced to go to a school where I had no friends. My perceived oppression was increased, for not only had I lost my cousin, but, at the time, North was a school I viewed as full of "gangsters" and "nerds."

As freshman year dragged on, I decided to become involved in some school activities and open up my shy persona by making friends with people who shared my same dry sense of humor. Slowly, things began to fall into place, but I had only made baby steps regarding my growth. Isolating myself from everyone had marred me, and the sad truth was that I still didn't even know it.

Summer was my safe haven. Not only was I able to escape from school, but I was able to read, read, and read . . . whatever I wanted! The summer following my first year of high school was when I discovered Anthony Kiedis's *Scar Tissue*. This book brought to light the shades of gray in my attempts to improve myself. His words were emblazoned on my mind and in my heart as I recollect how, throughout my life, I have always worked alone, whether the outcome was to be a success or failure. Otherwise, I somehow felt like I'd be cheating.

Today, as a senior in high school, I am especially grateful that, although I work like this "most of the time," I now enjoy asking for the help of others, which was once something that made me feel distinctly uncomfortable. After reading *Scar Tissue,* I feel humbled. I understand that I can't relate to other people until I am certain of who I am, at least "most of the time." My personality and belief systems are strong, yet they are not unwavering. Yes, I am stubborn "most of the time," but I also have an active awareness of when I do not know it all and need help. My growth is not over, and I am continually learning to practice modesty, both as a means to improve myself and a way to connect with others. I work hard "most of the time," but am willing to take a break and laugh with my close friends. I help my parents with their business "most of the time," but still depart from my duties and spend time relaxing with a book of my own choosing. I am willing to give life my all. Most of the time.

Saad is attending the University of California, Berkeley, with plans of majoring in biological science. In his free time, Saad enjoys spending time with family and friends, and he also enjoys playing soccer and running. An interesting fact about him is his ability to socialize. Whether in the classroom or in line at a store, Saad always finds himself conversing with other people—sometimes as the comic relief or sometimes just as a new friend.

Good Is Good

by Stephanie Treen

From our earliest days of childhood, we read books and see movies with a similar storyline, where good conquers evil and the hero saves the day. It is engraved upon our minds that every story must have a happy ending, that good people will win and that evil people will pay for their crimes. But what if it's just a story and it's not really true? It is the shocking realization that this story is just fiction that can cause an optimistic child to turn bitter, to see life as something full of meaningless pain and discouragement.

My life has always been very blessed, and even when bad things happened, one thing I had was my faith. I always knew in my heart that things would eventually right themselves and I could not fathom that anything bad would last for long. When my best friend moved away from me at the end of elementary school, I believed that there had to be some way of getting her to come back to me. She insisted that there was no way she would ever be able to move back to Riverside and that I should just give up thinking about it. There was no convincing me, though. I had an overwhelming hope that even in a situation that seemed hopeless, there was a possibility.

Months later, my friend's father had a heart attack, and though he survived, her family decided it was best for her to go live with some extended family in Riverside. I believed that God had used a terrible event to make the world right again and bring my best friend back to me. I trusted God to take the grimmest situation and somehow turn it into something beautiful.

For years, this same pattern would continue. Whenever something went wrong, I would pray and wait, believing that the best and highest good would come to pass. Faith was the one thing I could always cling to, a hope for a better tomorrow. My world came crashing down during my senior year of high school, however, when my best friend, the person I cared so much about, was put in the hospital. They said she had had some kind of mental breakdown and no one could figure out what was wrong with her. At first, I had hope, even though I couldn't understand what was happening. I honestly expected it to just go away and become a distant memory that we would laugh about later. But month after month went by and my faith started slipping further and further away.

When my friend got out of the hospital almost six months later, she came to live with my family. Under a false perception, I believed that I could make it better, that I could help heal her. I believed I had enough hope and faith for the both of us. But all was shattered when I realized that everything that was happening to her was completely out of my control. I cried out to God, not seeing why this was happening or how anything good could ever come of this. At the time, there were no answers, just confusion and pain.

Eventually, she had to go back to the hospital. When she got out, she went to live in a group home. At last, she went home, and she's now living with her mother on the other side of the country. After more than a year of pain and fear, she has improved enormously. She is on the right medication and on a good path toward healing. But in a lot of ways, it feels like irreparable damage has been done to our friendship and my faith through this whole ordeal.

After my friend stopped living with me, my relationship with God went downhill and I started to think that my faith was dead. For a while, things continued on this way; I was not at all surprised when more and more things happened in my life that only brought additional pain and hardship. I no longer had predictions of the good that the near future would hold. I simply accepted that the bad in the world had finally found me and those I love, and it would not release its grasp.

Slowly, though, things started to heal inside of me. I can say with full confidence that C.S. Lewis was right when he said in his book *The Great Divorce* that "bad cannot succeed even in being bad as truly as good is good." Though nothing miraculous happened, and my situation has remained the same for the most part, I suppose something inside me has grown to realize that not all things that appear to be bad on the surface truly are bad. I may not have the answers to why certain things happen, but I do know that evil can never truly win. This belief and my renewed trust in God are the things that keep my head held high and my hope alive.

It has been a long journey to my new sense of hope, but one that, in retrospect, has been amazing and beautiful in its own way. Because of the evil that humans brought into the world, bad things will continue to happen, but evil can never truly succeed. Darkness will never conquer light. Maybe not every story will end with a prince riding off into the sunset and not every happy ending may seem like one at first. But even in the saddest of endings, bad will never succeed because it's enough for me to know that I have hope and faith in the possibility of good—at least enough for today.

Stephanie will graduate from the University of California, Davis, in three years with a major in sociology and a minor in dramatic arts. She aspires to be an elementary school teacher, and she also has a passion for dance. She has been active in UCD's Choreography Program, and in high school she was part of the Blue Star Regiment's Color Guard. Stephanie has been on four short-term mission trips to Nicaragua and two to Nageezi, New Mexico.

Gone Away

by Akhila Pamula

The soft pitter-patter of the rain has a calming effect as I
gaze out of the large windows of my new living room into
the courtyard. The floor is still littered with boxes of every
shape and size, the cream-colored walls naked, begging for
accessories to adorn their bare faces. *I hate moving.* I scan
the red-brick path, framed by perfectly trimmed bushes,
water accumulating in the bowl-shaped yellow tulips that
surround a white metal bench sitting at the end of the lane.
A smile creeps onto my face as I flash back to my childhood
backyard, the green grass tickling my feet, the voices of my
parents and my brother echoing in my mind like a dream.
I close my eyes and picture the white bench that still sits in
the shade against the wall in the backyard. It has been every
possible color—green to gray, completely bare to multicolored, all due to my brief love affair with acrylic paints. It has
persevered through the unbearably hot desert summers,

the brief yet powerful rainstorms, and the shallow frost of winter. Though slightly rusty, it has always been there, my throne on lazy Sunday afternoons. As I reminisce, I realize just how long it has been since I have been back home, and the tears trickling down my cheeks mirror the raindrops rolling down the window.

I left home for college at the age of 17. While most of my friends were also moving out of the house to begin this journey, I took it to the extreme, moving over 3,000 miles away to the opposite coast. While my friends could drive home on a moment's notice, I had to commit to a six-hour plane ride; visiting home was a luxury. Yet I felt confident that I could thrive. I had always been extremely independent, balancing school with hours of extracurricular dance and orchestra rehearsals while maintaining a vibrant social life. During high school, if I was lucky, I would see my parents before heading to bed, and so I found it an exciting new challenge to move somewhere where I would be forced to become even more independent and essentially start over. Yes, I would be stripped of that security blanket of family and friends, but after all, they would all just be a quick phone call away, right?

The first few months were torture. I never realized how much I would miss my family. We lived under the same roof, and even if we didn't always get along or have conversations every day, the mere sight of them was enough to keep me grounded and happy. I no longer had that. Feelings of guilt would bubble up in my stomach, a constant ache. I knew that my family, though supportive, wasn't exactly thrilled with my decision to go so far away. My younger brother was only 13 years old and at a critical point in his life, facing the transition from being a carefree boy to a wily teenager. I felt guilty not being there to guide him through the tangled ropes of middle school. I can still see the look of sadness in his eyes as he left on the plane back to California and realized that this dorm room was my new home, a home far away from him. And though I knew that he needed to grow up and learn to navigate without me being there to coddle him, it was hard to see him go.

My parents knew that my decision had merit: I was accepted into medical school right out of high school, a feat that would save me years of extra school and tuition. My father tried to keep me home by promising me a car, an apartment, and more freedom if I just stayed local; he did not want his daughter facing the challenges of the real world so far away. My mother was more understanding, but she was dealing with the stress of being a newly diagnosed diabetic. Her diabetes was not under control and the complications of the disease were making her life more and more uncomfortable. I used my feelings of guilt and my longing for home, though, to fuel my fire. I needed to do well and make a name for myself so I *could* come back to California, so I *could* take care of my mother, guide my brother, and be my father's little girl again.

In one of my favorite books, *The House on Mango Street*, Esperanza realizes that as much as she wants to distance herself from Mango Street, she grew up there and it will always be a part of her. She writes about her experiences in order to forge a relationship between herself and her community. While still maintaining her own voice and identity, she knows she must remember her roots.

I'm not going to lie. Like Esperanza, I do not plan on settling in my hometown when I finish medical school. Yet I will never forget how that town shaped me: the diverse groups of people I met and grew up with who helped me learn to understand and to relate to my new friends today,

and to my patients in the future. The experiences I have had made me a strong, perseverant, and independent woman. My parents live there. My roots are there. And just like Esperanza says, "I have gone away to come back. For the ones I left behind." And so I will go back and live close enough so that, on a whim, I'll be able to swing by and rest on that bench in my backyard, with my father, my mother, and my brother sitting right next to me, shaded from the familiar California sun.

Akhila graduated as an International Baccalaureate diploma recipient and went on to earn a B.S. in biology from Rensselaer Polytechnic Institute. Akhila is currently a student at Albany Medical College. Along with being involved with scientific research, she is deeply involved in a teaching program that focuses on at-risk children in the community. In her spare time, she enjoys exploring and eating her way along the East Coast and sleeping in.

The Whole Damn Bunch

by Michelle Lu

Teenagers can be downright mean. Rumors and gossip spread like wildfire, and many teenagers stress over social issues more than over academic problems. I remember my freshman and sophomore years, in particular; I put a ton of thought into every single word that someone said to me or about me. It seems ridiculous, looking back, to think how I would overreact and worry about what everyone said regarding me or my opinions, because thinking about it so much made me a miserable person. I would come home from school depressed and moody. I knew deep inside that this had to stop before it ruined me. I slowly tried to tune out all the negative comments that people said about me, but it wasn't easy.

One instance that made me realize how little power I had over what people said was when I heard that certain people believed that I cheated on my schoolwork. People felt these comments were justified, for how else could I be getting such high marks on my work? Their opinion of me stung because I knew that I was able to achieve good scores on tests without having to look at anyone's paper or getting a copy of the test. After having the remark linger in my head for a few days, I realized that whatever people thought about me was up to them. What mattered most was that I knew deep inside that I wasn't a cheater. It occurred to me, then, that there would always be people out there who would be jealous and try to shake me up with their stupid remarks, but only I had the power to let them.

During the summer before my senior year, I stayed at home a lot and watched quite a bit of tennis. I was pretty sour on most of my friends from school and took a break from the social scene. Although it sounds boring, I am proud to say that these two simple activities changed my life. When I watched my idol, Roger Federer, lose his Wimbledon crown to Rafael Nadal, I cried, I complained, and I basically lost the will to do anything for several days. What hurt me more than his loss, though, was the negative media and criticism of Roger by his fans. It angered me how they said that Federer should think about retiring and how the younger players would soon take over. In my head, I kept thinking how Federer must have felt about all of these people, especially the fans who once claimed to love him and were now trashing his career.

Just as talk about the end of Federer's career became unbearably loud, he silenced everyone by winning the US Open, the last grand slam of the year. Federer's ability to end all the criticism and focus on his own business helped me see that as long as I believed in myself, nothing else mattered.

Later in my senior year, I would remember a quote I'd read in American Literature the previous year. The pettiness had crept back into friendships as everyone was vying for just the right acceptance letter from just the right college, and it reminded me of something from F. Scott Fitzgerald's *The Great Gatsby*. The book's narrator, Nick, saw Gatsby's grief at his rejection by the very people he most wanted to accept and love him. Nick told him, "You're worth the whole damn bunch put together." I could relate to those words. Once again, I saw it all so clearly. It really didn't matter if Federer or I fit in with a crowd that didn't want us. We were worth more than all of them put together! I kept telling myself I wouldn't see them anymore after high school, anyway. But I was no longer willing to let their harsh criticism hurt me. Now it's a quote I refer to whenever I am bothered by any hurtful remark that I know isn't true.

I am proud to say that, although I have not perfected the art of tuning out negative comments completely, I have gotten quite good at it. Having the ability to use discretion regarding what I give credence to or what I ignore has helped me focus primarily on my academics. This quality helped me become one of the five salutatorians at graduation, and I'm finding that I am surrounded by fewer acquaintances, but by more authentic friends. Now my friends come to me for advice on how to deal with the same kinds of issues I used to face. I have been given a gift, an essential life lesson through books and also through sports. Though it was painful to go through that summer of feeling jilted and alone, it is a joy for me to pass on some of the words I live by to the people I care about.

Michelle attends the University of California, Riverside, after having graduated as a salutatorian of her class. She hopes to attend Boston University School of Medicine to become a pediatric cardiologist. Michelle was a member of her high school's tennis team for four years and a team captain during her senior year. As a child, Michelle loved dogs and spent hours studying all the different breeds. In the future, she hopes to help shelters find loving homes for as many dogs as possible.

Honest Doubt

by Yadira Navarro

I'm thinking that I'm going to have to freewrite this because that's the only way that anything is really going to come out without me wanting to stop and hide what I'm really feeling. I mean, stream-of-consciousness writing is the only way that talking about my grandpa ever really comes out how I want it to, because I don't get to stop to edit myself; anyway, I'm rambling, even now, just trying to avoid writing this, but it's time, so I'm just going to do it. I'm not sure if it'll be any good, but here goes.

Are you ready? Well, my grandfather was the greatest man that I've ever known, the best man, the smartest man, and the kindest man. So when he died, I didn't know what to do with myself. A death in the family is always bad, but my grandfather's dying was heavy—not like the saying they used in the '70s—heavy like gravity pulling me into the earth, pinning me to the ground. It was like a vacuum, a machine that always sucks up everything you don't want it to, like the bobby pins that just happen to fall out of your hair, and then you can't ever get them back. My grandfather's dying was like getting locked out of the house in the rain, knowing your parents won't be home for hours and you have no choice but to sit on the porch and wait, wait it out until time passes and there is relief.

That's how much I cried that night, like an afternoon of rain, and when I woke up in the morning, I knew I had to go to school. I had to go because school was my only real distraction and if I went to school, then I didn't have to think about how my grandpa's dead and he's never coming back. I didn't have to think about how he might not be in heaven because maybe there is no such thing as heaven. And after all, who could I admit this to? My parents? Never! My self-assured friends? Of course not. But I finally had to face what I've always doubted, always, and what I've never been able to say aloud: I really don't think I've ever believed in a God or an Almighty or even that I'm agnostic. I've always been full of doubt, and that's regarding everything, not just religion. I doubt everything.

Moreover, I've always doubted whether the decisions I've made are the right ones or if I'm on the right path. I've doubted whether my decision to stay at home for college was the smarter thing to do. I've agonized over whether the job I'm aiming for is really what I want to do for the rest of my life or if I'm just fooling myself. After all, the rest of my life is a long time.

When my grandpa died, I just kept doubting and doubting and wondering where he was, really. Was he up in the clouds or was he just cold, lying in the ground and beginning to rot? And since there were no answers, I went to school that morning with my head racing and my heart breaking.

It's so funny the way things work out, because that morning when I walked into class, that was the day we started reading *In Memoriam* by Tennyson, and I remember thinking to myself how unbelievably lucky I was that day. Was it possible that the stars were aligned and the cosmos made this work out? Because whoever planned this class, on this day, with this reading selection, was definitely trying to make me grieve—make me face my doubts when I completely didn't want to—by making me read this poetry by this stupid dead author named Tennyson. And you know what was super strange? I even have doubts about the day I had to start reading this book, because that's the day I really started to think that maybe things do happen for a reason; and even though I read *In Memoriam* for the sake of my grade in the class, and for the sake of Tennyson and his dead friend, it started to feel like I was reading for the sake of my sanity, and I read and read and read this book like no other book I had ever read before. I read that book until I felt it in my soul, and it helped me cry the way I needed to cry, and it helped me understand that doubt is okay. Because if Tennyson could write an entire one hundred pages in an "a b, a b" rhyme scheme and say that doubt is okay, then I knew that others must feel doubt the way I have throughout my whole life.

For the first time ever, I felt like my doubts were okay—in fact, even better than okay, because at least I was being honest. Tennyson wrote that "There lives more faith in honest doubt, believe me, than in half the creeds," and when I read this quote, I was so glad that I was at home and not at school because I started to bawl, sobbing out loud and messy-like, because that's when I knew that being unsure was okay. I knew, then, that it didn't matter where my grandfather was. All that mattered was that I knew I loved him and that he would always be with me. I knew right then that it was okay for me to be unsure of what I want to do with my life and that it was okay for me to doubt if there's a God—because until he decides to show up, nobody can know for sure. I knew then that doubt is okay.

That day, I embraced my doubt instead of feeling shame from its presence. I saw that it is actually better than blind faith, because doubt is smart; it's smart enough to make us question everything. Question the common question or the conventional question, question authority, and question the norm.

I saw a bumper sticker once that suggested that to doubt is to wonder and to wonder is to try to give every side of a story the chance it deserves. Now, when people ask me what I want to be when I grow up, I can honestly say that I don't know and just walk away with my head held high. Now, when I get scolded by the people who have their lives planned out to the minute, I sometimes actually feel proud that I don't know, because my plan has room for growth; it has room to develop; it has room for changes and the curveballs that life chucks at me. I'm finally okay with saying, simply, that I just don't know. Does anybody?

Yadira attends the University of California, Riverside, majoring in English and philosophy. At UCR she has worked as a peer mentor, an orientation counselor, and chief of staff in the Office of External Affairs. She will attend graduate school for communications and advertising, where she will blend her passions for writing and commerce. She continues to grow up in both Southern California and Mexico City.

Nobody

by Zerka Wadood

Growing up, I lived in a very sheltered household. My parents had just moved to America from Pakistan, and I was the first child, the first daughter, in a new country and a new culture. They wanted to protect me and make sure I grew up with the right values, but in doing so, they didn't allow me to really experience life. My days consisted of going to school, coming home and doing homework, maybe watching a little TV, reading, and then doing it all over again. I wasn't allowed to go out with friends because my parents didn't want my impressionable personality to be corrupted by a culture that they didn't really understand, nor wanted to understand. They just wanted me to be safe. By protecting me from perceived evils, they made sure I was always safe, but I stayed hidden in the shadows. No one really knew who I was. I was just the "smart girl" in school. I wasn't anyone's friend, not even my own.

When I started high school, I got a taste of what being my own person was like. I saw a life where people wanted to talk to me because of who I was and not because I knew the right answers. I started talking to people and making friends, and I loved the attention. However, I got a bit overzealous. In order to keep the attention and friends, I became someone I wasn't. I would do anything I could to fit in and be liked. Though I am thankful that I never had big problems, like drugs or absent parents, during this time I stepped much farther out of my comfort zone than ever before. It was different and exciting, having something to do after school besides homework.

Somewhere between making friends and breaking through the shell I had been in since I was young, I realized I was starting to lose myself. I didn't agree with the morals of the people with whom I was hanging out, but I was overlooking that to stay out of obscurity. I was constantly fighting an internal battle between doing what I thought was right and gaining the approval of my friends. At first, I learned to quiet that little voice in my head because I was having fun and I was happy. I hushed that voice into silence.

When it was time to decide what I wanted to do after high school, I decided I wanted to get as far away as I could. I had gotten a glimpse of freedom in high school and wanted to experience what life would be like without anyone telling me when I could go out and what I could do. I wanted to be free.

So I chose a college away from home and I was ready to jump right back into the same type of friendships and pick up right where I left off in high school. But this time something was different. I met people who wanted to get to know me and be my friend, people I didn't have to follow around all the time. It seemed easier being friends with these people. When I was around them, there was no little voice in my head anymore. I resisted giving up my old friends for a while because I didn't want to lose any of the attention, but I soon realized that the number of people I could call my friends didn't matter, because most of them *weren't* my friends. They were just people who used me, and my eagerness to be liked, to their advantage. My new friends liked me for who I was and didn't want to change anything.

I started going home more, and I saw that my family always loved me for who I was and only wanted the best for me. Yes, they were protective, but they also understood an idea that John Steinbeck explored in *Of Mice and Men*. A character named Crooks says, "S'pose you didn't have nobody. . . . A guy needs somebody—to be near him. A guy goes nuts if he ain't got nobody." I couldn't agree more. I had experienced what it was like not having anyone to talk to, and it was very lonely indeed. The thing I hadn't realized, however, was that I didn't need to be liked by everybody. All that mattered was that I had a few people who loved and cared about me, people who would be near when I needed them. Even if it was only one person, if he or she actually cared about me, it was worth more than many friends who weren't true.

I have finally come to appreciate my family and the few people I now know I can call my real friends. With them, I can be myself. I don't have to change anything. I don't have to fight the internal battle of right versus wrong anymore. With this newfound self-acceptance, I can finally grow as a person and be there when my family and friends need me. I'm somebody.

Zerka graduated from the University of California, Los Angeles, where she majored in biomedical engineering. She now attends Saba University School of Medicine, where she is pursuing her dream of becoming a surgeon. Zerka enjoys playing badminton with her friends and competes in several tournaments each year. She also takes photographs and enjoys spending time with her three sisters.

And So...

Questions for Reflection, Discussion, and Writing

Have you ever considered what it would be like to go through life without anyone to share it with? Do you feel like you have a close and reliable group of friends and loved ones, or do you often feel isolated? Humans are social creatures by nature, and most of us want to make connections with others. But it isn't always easy to build and maintain relationships, and it isn't always under our control. As you read the questions below, consider the ideas the essay writers in this section shared about their experiences with family, friends, and love.

Anthony shares his grief over losing a brother he never knew, and describes the way that loss motivates him to achieve big things in his life—for himself, but also for his parents. If you have brothers or sisters, what expectations do your parents have for you compared to your siblings? If you're an only child, do you feel that there's extra pressure on you? How do you feel about your family's expectations for you?

Jessica writes about her first love. What do you think about teenage love? If you've been in love, consider what that experience was like. Did adults view your relationship differently than you did, and, if so, how did that feel? Also consider how love can make someone better—or how it can have the opposite effect. What roles do love and romance—or the desire for them—play in your life and the lives of those around you?

Asma realizes that, in an effort to be liked by others, she developed more than one persona. Write about your own different selves, such as the person your family sees at home, the person you are with friends, and the person you are at school. Reflect on what would happen if you let all of your masks fall to the wayside and tried to be the same person with everyone. What, if anything, is stopping you from doing this?

Rachele talks about how her mother is an inspiration to her. Consider someone you know who has faced a physical or mental challenge that was beyond his or her control. How has this person inspired you? What challenges have you overcome in your own life, and how have they shaped your character?

Saad's essay explores the frightening experience of losing a family member to drug addiction. Reflect on the ways you escape when life becomes overwhelming. Have you ever indulged in a type of escape that was dangerous or unhealthy? Do you know anyone who has wrestled with addiction? Did that person overcome it, and, if so, how?

For *Stephanie,* watching her friend suffer from mental illness led her to doubt her own beliefs. Have you ever looked on as a loved one suffered from depression or some other illness? How does it feel when someone you care about is hurting? What can you do to help?

Akhila moved away from home in hopes of realizing her dream to become a doctor. Would you be willing to live far away from your family to pursue your dreams? If so, how do you think your family would react to your choice and absence? How would *you* feel? Consider the strengths you would need to be able to move away from home and make it on your own.

Like *Michelle,* you may have had to deal with others talking about you unkindly or judging you unfairly. How easy or difficult is it for you to let go of the things others say about you? How do other people's opinions of you affect the way you feel about yourself?

When *Yadira* was struggling with the pain of losing her grandfather and the doubts that this loss raised, she decided to let her mind and emotions wander freely as she expressed her pain on paper. Are there any major doubts that you hide because you're worried that others might judge you for them? If so, what are they? Have you ever used writing, art, music, or other expressions to let out your feelings? If so, how did that affect the way you felt? If not, how *do* you deal with difficult emotions?

Zerka finds herself moving away from some of the ideas that are important to her parents. Have you also found that your family's value system and beliefs do not always match yours as you become a young adult? When there are differences, how do you think you and your family can bridge this gap?

Part 3
Essays on Hard Times and Hope

"You are braver than you believe, stronger than you seem, and smarter than you think."
—Christopher Robin in A.A. Milne's *Winnie the Pooh*

The World Belongs to You

by Nooreya Shenghur

Nine. For some reason, the number nine has always played some significance in my life. In 1989, I was the ninth born in a family of ten girls, giving me a grand total of, yes, nine sisters. I was even dubbed with the nickname "Number Nine." Apparently, family friends were having trouble keeping track of all of our names. Living in a small house with my nine sisters and parents was the only life I knew, and I would not have had it any other way. To me, it was normal to share a bedroom and wear hand-me-downs.

To the outsider, it might have seemed that I had a skewed sense of normalcy, but I was oblivious to it. Each morning, I'd wake up to the aroma of my mom's scrambled eggs and potatoes with grilled hot dog bits mixed in, a shared favorite of our family. As my dad ate, I'd watch him pour on what seemed like a pound of hot chilies and hot sauce. I marveled at how the beads of sweat rolled down from his hairline, down the subtle crevices of his cheek, and off of his face. Afterward, I would stand on the toilet seat and watch my dad get ready for work, in hopes that he'd hand me the razor and let me help him shave his beard. My mother would smile and tell me to count my blessings, but I never understood exactly what she meant.

These were my daily activities most mornings, until the number nine decided to reappear in my life. In April of 1999, when I was nine years old, my father was murdered. *Murdered.* I had heard this word before, but never imagined I would feel its devastating blow and backlash.

In the following months, I'd wake up and run to my parents' room, half-expecting the usual morning activities, but was dismayed each time I found the bed empty. Even to this very day, I have vivid dreams that my father is alive, and I am robbed again and again when I wake up. At the time, I thought I understood the severity of this tragedy, but in retrospect, I realize that I didn't really grasp it at all.

Over the years, dismay grew into anger at the fact that I did not understand so many things. I did not understand why this was the lot for my family. I could never quite understand why the pain of losing my father never really went away, but how instead I grew almost numb to the dull pain that just lingered in the background. I had known my father for only nine short years, so growing up as a teenager, I could never understand what it was like to have a male figure in my life. Often, I'd whisper "Dad" silently to myself, but the word felt foreign on my tongue.

Perplexities plagued me, but I repressed them. Any preconceived philosophies I held about family life were bro-ken. My father had been my family's rock. When he died, any semblance of my old life died with him. Everything that was commonplace to me had changed, and I remained confused and angry. I felt like I was robbed of everything I had held dear, and I was left with nothing but perpetual trials. I could not wrap my mind around having "nothing." I needed more; I needed answers. I asked futile questions whose answers were impossible to find, igniting an inferno that engulfed my heart and thoughts, a flame I desperately needed to douse.

When I read James Frey's book *A Million Little Pieces*, his words spoke to me. Something tugged at my heart when I read, "Be content with what you have and take joy in the way things are. When you realize you have all you need, the world belongs to you. . . . If you understand that all things change constantly, there is nothing you will hold on to." These words latched onto my mind and settled into my heart. I could hear my anger call a ceasefire. The inferno was doused.

So here I am, years later, and I am not sure why my life turned out the way it did. How different would it have been if my father were still alive? What would have happened if my mother had allowed herself to climb into the darkness of the burdening shadows cast by her 10 daughters she had to raise alone? I won't ever know the answers to these questions, but I have other things. In fact, I have all I need in life—maybe not necessarily everything I want, but definitely what I need. Frey's words have brought me this new understanding and solace.

Over the years, I had forgotten to count my blessings, though there have been so many. Today, when I look back on my life, I feel content. Reflections of my childhood, which once seemed dim, have been illuminated. I have become a firm believer that everything, no matter how big or small, fantastic or appalling, happens for a reason. Instead of taking the easy way out and using my tragedy as an excuse for failure, I have used it as a reason to succeed, to gather a new life instead of trying to put together the broken pieces of my old one, and I take joy in the way things turned out.

The number nine reappeared in my life once more and brought more change, an exciting and welcome change. In 2009, I received my bachelor's degree at 19 years old and I now look forward to what else the number nine has in store for me. Although I know more trials are bound to come, today I understand that this is part of life. The only question I ask now is, "What more do I need if the world already belongs to me?" The answer is, thankfully, nothing.

In 1982, Nooreya's parents emigrated from Afghanistan to the United States. She and her nine sisters all earned college degrees. Nooreya earned a bachelor's degree in business administration at the University of California, Riverside, and works in business development and marketing at a civil engineering company. She plans to attend graduate school. She also enjoys traveling and trying new adventures. Nooreya owes her success and perseverance to her mother, who selflessly strived for the best for Nooreya and her nine sisters.

Only a Half Step

By Roxana Mohrdar

Until a few weeks ago, I never had a true understanding of what it meant to live. I mean, I know that life is precious and we are always told to appreciate everything in our lives. However, to "know" something and to really understand it are two entirely different things.

I had spent five weeks, two of which I can't even remember, in the hospital for a bacterial infection that nearly killed me. It was clear to me before I got any explanation that something serious had happened. Whenever a doctor or someone who had seen me before I regained consciousness stopped by after I woke up, they made comments like, "Wow, you were really knocking on the doors of heaven for a while," which didn't make things much easier while being strapped up to a ventilator, fed through a gastric tube, and having no ability to ask questions. It turned out that the bacteria from my throat had infected my jugular vein and gone global (turning my body septic), and had moved from pneumonia to a little-known disease called Lemierre's syndrome. I needed life support, five chest tubes, a couple of transfusions, and a surgery to remove part of my jugular vein just to stay alive. To the great chagrin of my vanity, the doctors pumped me up with 160 pounds of fluid, making me about 300 pounds. You should see the lovely stretch marks it left on my body and my pride!

What was really relevant, though, was what I discovered after I woke up. After flipping out that I was on a ventilator and being told how long I had been sedated, a thought came to my mind. I could have died and not known it. All my life, I had been so afraid of dying, but all of a sudden, death seemed too simple. It was subtle and devious, but simple, and possibly the easiest thing we ever do.

This whole ordeal came out of the blue. It started off as a common flu and quickly spiraled into something out of my control. I'd heard adults preach about living life to the fullest, but, like most teenagers, I would just nod and brush it away. After all, the day before going to the hospital, I was outside, lying in the sun. I had no idea that the next day I would be put on life support. Life was so fragile but, unfortunately, that was hard for me to really comprehend until I had almost lost it.

There were moments when I wanted out. The ventilator was horrible. I was literally struggling for every breath. My lungs felt so weak, and no matter how hard I tried, I couldn't get enough air. Every day there was a new challenge that cost me almost every ounce of energy, and I felt trapped in a surreal nightmare. I started to withdraw; I didn't know what else to do. It was that or tearing off all the cords and running out the front door. I became indifferent. I stopped trying to communicate and just lay there like a pathetic bag of potatoes. I was that way for a couple of weeks, but as

soon as I saw my brother in the room, I remembered my
life outside the hospital. I remembered how we would often
fight, but how I could never care for anyone as much as I
cared for him. I saw the sadness and worry in his eyes as he
forced on his famous smile. He saved me. He gave me the
energy and motivation to fight harder.

In his novel *The Grapes of Wrath,* John Steinbeck writes,
"This you may say of man—when theories change and
crash, when schools, philosophies, when narrow dark alleys
of thought, national, religious, economic, grow and disinte-
grate, man reaches, stumbles forward, painfully, mistakenly
sometimes. Having stepped forward, he may slip back, but
only half a step, never the full step back." Steinbeck is right
when he makes the point that even though some events
appear as failures, they can still be successes. It may at first
not seem so, but a failure's purpose is to be learned from
and corrected in the future. I got a second chance, a chance
to try again and improve myself. Even though what happened to me seemed devastating at the time, it has been one
of the most productive parts of my life. Without this experience, it's sad to say, I wouldn't have the same perspective
on life.

My relationship with my brother was horrible but now
I would give my life for him. Sure, we will argue and fight
again, but it will be better—not perfect, just better. I fought
for that half a step harder than I hope I ever have to fight
for anything again. It was painful, but now that I have won,
I feel so alive, so strong, so open to all of life's gifts.

The fight is all about motivation. It is amazing how
much one's mentality affects the results of a situation.
Within the second day of having this rejuvenated feeling,
I qualified for a swallowing test. When the speech thera-
pist started me off with some ice and cold water, I began
to cry. I cried from the sheer ability to do something I had

always taken for granted. Swallowing, by far, was what I had missed the most. I can tell you now that a gastric tube just doesn't cut it. I learned how important and valuable the small things are, such as walking, driving, and lying outside in the sun. I didn't realize how little I appreciated my body and the things and people around me until I had almost lost them all.

Within three weeks of waking up, I was able to return home, home to my bed, home to my friends and family, who loved me throughout this ordeal. To say that I did it alone would be untrue. Everyone needs people to inspire them, support them, and remind them of hope. I had no idea how much my parents truly loved me, and not for one minute was I alone. They stood by, doing everything imaginable to help me get better. I will never forget it and I will never forget that fight. It built endurance, and by endurance, I don't mean the kind that helps a person finish a marathon, but rather the endurance to face any challenge. I feel stronger, as though I can handle any difficulty, because I have already hit rock bottom, and nothing feels better than getting back up.

Roxana attends the University of California, Riverside, and plans on graduating with a bachelor's degree in neuroscience. She wants to use that degree to go to medical school and hopes to become a neurosurgeon. She is fluent in French and understands Farsi. She also has a passion for art, traveling, and reading.

Words Are No Good

by John Joanino

I remember walking out of our hotel room and into the lobby for the same old complimentary continental breakfast that I had eaten every morning for the past few weeks. My parents did not qualify for an apartment, so this was our home. I remember telling my mother to pick me up from school late because I didn't want anybody to see our old white minivan roll into the school parking lot. We eventually moved into a cramped one-bedroom apartment, where my sister and I slept on the floor, layering blankets on the thin carpet so that it didn't feel so hard.

My life has been full of obstacles and unusual circumstances. Some of them are so painful that I try to hide them in the deepest regions of my memory. Toward the beginning of my freshman year, I caught a close family member just seconds before she was about to commit suicide. I remember crying for hours when my father told me he wished I had never been born. Often, my parents would exchange harsh words, usually because of the same issues: bills, food, more bills. But on the days when my sister and I heard the walls pound and plates shatter, we would hide in the corner and huddle together, scared for our lives. These are just a few of the memories that remain. Most of the others have faded, and it's probably for the best.

Nonetheless, the words of my father and mother continue to echo in my mind. They would reassure us that everything would be all right and tell us that soon we wouldn't have to worry about where we would spend the night. But my sister and I always saw the despair in their faces as they struggled with the words, trying to mask the fact that we were living on a thread. In *As I Lay Dying*, William Faulkner wrote, "I learned that words are no good; that words don't ever fit even what they are trying to say." I've lived most of my childhood hearing and wanting to believe my parents' empty words, but I've grown to learn that they mean nothing without the intent to act upon them. Words don't stop the pain, pay the rent, or heal the scars.

Over and over again, my mom and dad would find a temporary solution, and each time they told themselves they could fix their money problems with gambling. Ironically, their solution was the root of all of our problems. My sister and I would sit in our makeshift living room, starving, while our parents searched for that magical "Royal Flush" or the lucky "777" a couple of hours away. But most of the time, they weren't magical or lucky. We would get evicted again and move to another apartment down the street. This wasn't very difficult, considering that all of our belongings could be packed into a single car.

One day, my dad got on an airplane to visit my uncle in the Philippines and what was supposed to be a few days turned into years and I haven't seen him since. So now we stay with my grandma every summer to save rent money. In 2008, our storage was robbed and everything from our legal documents to precious family albums was stolen. I grew depressed and began to feel utterly helpless. Those nights on the cold floor when I'd sing songs and watch the stars with my sister bolstered me, though, and became close to my heart. They reminded me that there was someone who had shared my pain and that this life was worth living. Furthermore, I refused to let my problems cloud my focus on the prize of a good education. On those days that it was almost too painful to wake up and go to school, I still knew that an education was my only way out.

Currently, I live with my mother; her social security benefits are our only means of income. So many different obstacles could have hindered my ability to perform my best in school, but I've discovered that problems are just that: problems. And words, no matter how wise or comforting, are just that: words. It's what I do with my problems and the words that matter.

As it turned out, my circumstances and adversities became just as motivating as they were hindering. Today, the words of William Faulkner remind me that overcoming my problems does not start by telling myself that they don't exist, but challenges me with what I will do after I face them. My life is defined not by my problems, but by my growth in overcoming them. It is defined not by my words, but by my actions. Pursuing an education and being a leader has set me on the path to a future that leads away from the pain of my difficult upbringing. As I look back, I wonder what kind of person I would be had I not faced and overcome those obstacles. I am proud to be the young man I am today. I cannot change the past and I'll never forget it. I'll simply take it with me and shape a better future, not because of what I say but because of what I do.

John is pursuing a sociology major and public affairs minor at the University of California, Los Angeles. He submitted this piece of writing as his supplemental essay in his UCLA application He sits on the University of California Student Association Board of Directors as the campus organizing director for UCLA. He was named one of Riverside's Top 25 Remarkable Teens in the category of Civic Involvement and continues that dedication as a resident assistant with the UCLA Office of Residential Life. He loves theater, music, art, student government, and politics.

Nothing Beats a Failure

by Archeé McDonald

As a young girl, I experienced the true meaning of pain and suffering. At the age of eight, I lost the center of my world, my mother, to renal kidney failure, an incurable and terrible disease that shuts down the functions of the kidneys slowly and, eventually, completely. I watched this strong and amazing woman give everything she had as she deteriorated in front of my eyes. I am grateful for the time she was here, though, and her life taught me a valuable lesson. I learned that I should never regret any decision if it's something I really believe in, and that trying is all part of the success no matter the outcome. Whether I win or lose, I learned not to let anyone stop me from doing what I set out to do.

As a motherless child, I was a young girl who became a young woman searching for an answer to her emptiness. In middle school, I tried to put those lonely and difficult years behind me and coped with the loss of my mother by eagerly tackling various goals to secure my future. I found motivation in remembering how my mother would boast about my good grades, but soon after starting middle school, my behavior wavered from day to day. One moment I was an angel, but the next, depression would fuel a terrible wrath. Due to my emotional instability, I was forced to move to a home where I now reside.

In high school, I moved back into a comfort zone where my intelligence was appreciated and encouraged. My mind was both my strength and weakness, for it held the most sacred memories of my mother. Through these memories, I created mountains of poems and writing pieces that I shared with both my teachers and friends. But internally, I fought the expectation of being labeled as a poet or an artist when I just wanted to write to release my pain so I could move on. In an attempt to embrace life, I accepted an invitation to try out for volleyball at my high school. I stepped into the gym with no experience of the sport or its fundamentals, but somehow made the summer team.

During that summer, I discovered that it was not the game that pulled me in, but the relief of knowing I had someone to encourage me. As my skills improved, I began to hear people cheer for me. This feeling was often overwhelming, as it drew me back to the days when my mom would boast about my accomplishments. Every time I felt the game was getting too hard to handle, some of my teammates would stand by with open arms to embrace me. I finally figured out that volleyball was the connection between holding on to what was left of my sanity and giving up on life. Though we won only two games that season, I had found another home to belong to. But my struggles weren't over.

Going into my junior year of high school, I had purposely chosen the sport of volleyball because both of my sisters had played basketball when they were younger. When I made the volleyball team for the first time as a rookie player, I was really proud of myself. I found out quickly, though, that girls could be vindictive and they would try to eliminate anyone they felt threatened their time in the limelight. For weeks, I was the new girl who was constantly plotted against because they assumed I was weak. And in the beginning, I *was* vulnerable and let these girls' opinions make me almost think that I wanted to quit. Almost.

Though my stamina and skill were on the low end of the scale for a great portion of the season, I could see that all that mattered to my coach was that I put in my best effort. My way of thinking was not anywhere near her positive attitude. I thought about how much easier my life would be without volleyball if I just quit and focused on school completely. I almost talked myself into being a failure because I found it easier not to work so hard, but I realized that I would have regretted running away. I recalled a line from *Can't Stop the Shine*, a book that I had read recently. In it, Joyce Davis wrote that "nothing beats a failure but a try." And so, in the memory and honor of my mother, I decided to go forward with volleyball. More importantly, I decided to stay true to a personal goal that I watched my mother make: to try no matter the outcome.

Today, I know that volleyball keeps me level; it keeps me grounded; it keeps me close to the words of my mother. When I'm in the off-season, I notice that my mind is weaker and more willing to conform to my pessimistic thoughts of giving up on life. Though the author's words of encouragement were from one sister to another about entering a talent show at their high school, and my story was about volleyball, they were just like my mother's words of advice. Even when I faced pessimism and criticism from my opponents, I never let them hinder me from trying.

Now that I am back in season, my mind is in training as well as my body. I no longer even consider the phrase "I can't." Ultimately, I have been successful, for I've kept up my grades and have made the varsity team for my senior year. I don't regret anything. I stared failure in the face and fought its unwavering attempts to bind me on its emotional roller coaster. By simply trying, I beat failure, and I bet my mom would be so proud of me if she could see me now.

Archeé grew up in Southern California, in both Perris and Riverside. She and her father share the same birthday, which is also her parents' wedding anniversary. Archeé had an especially close relationship with her mother. After being in the college-bound support program Advancement Via Individual Determination (AVID) for three years, Archeé began attending Clark Atlanta University in 2012.

The Rest of the World

by Kaylee Rangel

He had finally come home and their loud voices rang throughout the house like a fire alarm in a crowded class-room. I sat in the hallway with my baby brother nestled in my arms and my little sister crying on my shoulder, her arms around my waist. We were scared. The raging fight my parents had started that night seemed to be the worst one yet, and we didn't know what to make of it.

I sat, lightly pounding my head against the wall, as if to banish the thoughts that were swirling in my mind, the made-up scenarios of how this fight would end, visions that I seemed to see over and over. Would it end with a trip to the hospital? A death? I was becoming absolutely deliri-ous. I turned my head and saw my mom coming down the hall, while pushing my dad away. Was he actually trying to make up with her again? I was supposed to be able to look up to him, but I could only look away as he started on his never-ending list of excuses that we all had heard so many times before. It turns out that this time, he was in Las Vegas spending money and pursuing yet another woman who wasn't my mother. It seemed as though this was going to be the end. But then again, it always seemed this way.

"I've had enough!" my mother yelled as she stormed past us and started throwing things into any bag within reach. I started to stand slowly, rocking my fussy brother and rubbing my little sister's back and whispering comforting things to them. Their hiccups made my mother and me both smile as our eyes met, but we didn't mention how or why they were caused, because this would ruin the only happy moment in this house of sorrow. I turned and snickered at my father's bewildered expression and outstretched arms. Through my young eyes, he was getting exactly what he deserved. I thought of all the dance recitals he had missed and the school assemblies I had wasted, searching for his face in the crowd while he was busy impressing someone else's children and lying next to another woman in her bed. He had been given so many chances, but his chances had run out.

I remember staying at my aunt's house, playing with my cousins and almost forgetting all of my worries. Almost. After we had a day of playing, my mother called us inside and sat down. The frown on her lips and the shadow in her eyes made me shudder. She saw me notice this and offered a weak smile, and I wondered if she would ever smile again, the kind of smile that comes from the inside, not just one that she would wear to cover her pain. She blurted out, "Me and Daddy are getting a divorce."

"A divorce!" I cried. "What's going to happen to us?"

She went on to explain that she and my father were no longer going to be together because they didn't get along anymore. She said that he had made some bad decisions and she couldn't live with him any longer, but we would stay with her.

For a long time since then, I have had to live with looks of pity and sadness from many people in my life. They felt sorry for me, having to live with a family that had been split up. But those who looked at me this way didn't know the whole story. As strange as this sounds, I felt like Bella did in Stephenie Meyer's book *Twilight*, when she got similar looks of disdain and pity. She admitted, "Sometimes I wondered if I was seeing the same things through my eyes that the rest of the world was seeing through theirs." That's exactly how I felt whenever I looked at my newly formed family.

Today, my mother is happy. I no longer have to hear her cry herself to sleep or watch her curvy figure become unhealthily skinny. Her smile reaches deep into her eyes and the only sound that can be heard throughout our house now is laughter. I have an amazing half-brother whose giggles fill me with joy, and my brother and sister enjoy life and no longer have to hide behind me. Others might wonder how I can see the good in a situation that might seem so dreadful. Yet these things never cross my mind, because I focus on the light that glows from inside, the smiles that cover my loved ones' faces, like diamonds in the sun. Like Bella, I see something so much more than others can see, and that's all that matters.

Kaylee attends the University of California, Riverside, majoring in anthropology and sociology. She spends her free time working, reading, and spending time with her family and friends, many of whom she developed a close bond with through the college-bound support program AVID. She continues to struggle with her relationship with her father, but still tries to make it work for the sake of her younger siblings.

Before I Met the Monster

by Krissie Gierz

All of us have our own monster. Something we are addicted to, something we are afraid of, something that we can't rid ourselves of or get away from—anything that takes up more of our lives than it should, whether we want it to or not. For some of us, that "something" is stealing, violence, gambling, drugs, alcohol, sex, or any kind of negative relationship with someone or something that is out of our control. It might be eating too much food or not eating any food, spending too much money or never spending any money at all, working all the time or never lifting a finger, being obnoxious or being obnoxiously nice, always being in control or always feeling out of control, constantly being around people or always being alone, going to the gym every day or not working out often enough, having unbounded self-confidence or unbounded self-loathing, having blind faith in a higher power or having a total lack of faith in everything, compulsively checking email, MySpace, Facebook, and Twitter, or proclaiming the evils of all things Internet-related.

Ellen Hopkins wrote in her book *Crank*, "Life was good before I met the monster. After, life was great. At least for a little while." I could totally relate. A slew of researchers and psychologists over the years have found ways to "fix" all of these monsters and have created a list of –isms: alcoholism, racism, sexism, consumerism, egoism, pessimism. Not one of us can say that we have never had to overcome some sort of addiction or have not had some kind of monkey on our backs. It seems to me that pretty much everyone has addictions, and everyone has the capability to overcome them. The only question is whether or not we want to overcome them.

I, of course, have my own personal monster. In fact, I would even go so far as to say that I have many of them. I love pretty, shiny, and expensive things that I don't need. I am compelled to put on makeup and do my hair before I show myself to the world. I am a comfort-eater and a chocolate junkie. I have a bad habit of criticizing other people for things I myself do. Even though I'm not entirely sure how to use them, I am almost never seen without my iPhone, iPod, or laptop. I am always connected in some way—my text messages, email, and Facebook are always the touch of a finger away.

The thing is, I know about all of these faults, but I don't feel entirely bad about any of them. Likewise, I don't think many people can look at themselves and not have a very similar list. Parents, teachers, and counselors always tell you that the only thing holding you back is yourself. My whole life, I have been told that I can do whatever I put my mind to. I have watched movies and listened to songs telling me that I can find my perfect Prince Charming and have three perfect children and have that perfect balance between my perfect family and my perfect dream job and that I can be perfectly happy if I only want it badly enough and work hard enough. As a consequence, I have become my biggest monster. I refuse to accept anything less than perfection. I am simply unable to. If I'm not good at a sport or a game or a class, I don't ever play that sport or game again and I never take a similar class. I would rather live in a world where I am good at everything I do or not do it at all.

Over the past couple of years, my perfectionism has come back to haunt me because my life is far from perfect. Among other things, I have been evacuated from my house in the San Bernardino Mountains because of six forest fires in the past five years. I have found out that my mom is sick and that there is nothing I can do to make her healthy again. I have seen my best friend go through her first quarter of college as a complete mess because she was drugged and sexually assaulted. All of these things have made me more thankful for what I have, and they have started what I like to think of as the beginning of the end.

My perfectionism and need for control have been shattered, and I am all right with that. I know that it won't be long before I find a new monster; I'm almost looking forward to getting a new monster to consume my life. I can last only so long filling the hole my perfectionism has left with chocolates and new shoes, and I'm hoping for something fun and helpful to catch my eye. Maybe I'll start memorizing the encyclopedia and writing it into songs on the guitar, or maybe I will find a connection between watching the news and eating chocolate ice cream.

To me, the worst thing that could happen to any of us would be looking back at our lives and having regrets because of our monsters. Life should not be lived in a constant pursuit of a new goal: graduating from high school, graduating from college, finding a job, getting married, having kids, and then watching our kids repeat the cycle all over again. Life, with all its heartaches and happiness, is a valuable entity in and of itself.

I want to live my life the way I want to live it, but the most important thing to me is recognizing what my monster is and finding a way to overcome it and continue on. At least until the next monster comes along.

Krissie attends the University of California, Los Angeles, as a biology major. She hopes to continue on to veterinary school. She grew up in the San Bernardino Mountains with her parents and older brother. Her parents moved to the United States from Germany in 1978, which means that Krissie has dual citizenship. She volunteers at Showcase Training Stables in Redlands and interns with the local veterinarian. She is also active as a volunteer both in the San Bernardino Mountains and Los Angeles.

My Mother Is a Fish

by Desirée Rogers

I was eight years old when I convinced myself that there had to be a God. There had to be a Heaven, a beautiful place where anything imaginable became possible. I convinced myself of this because if it was not true and angels did not exist, then my little sister did not exist anymore, either. God was real, Heaven was real, and my sister was not dead. She was just gone, temporarily. This was the only way I could shield myself from the devastation of losing my baby sister, who had barely seen two years. I tried to remove myself from my family's emotional tragedy, and then, since I was still young and alive, move on with my life.

It has been 12 years since her death, and I am now gripped tightly by the hands of reality. God, Heaven, and angels are not a part of this reality. My little sister is no more, and the two years I lived with her and loved her during my childhood remain in the past. It is rare that I am able to summon her face or remember her smell or recall the sound of her laugh. It is rarer, still, that I even try to remember. Some might disagree with my view and try to convince me that she's alive and well and with God; others might think it depressing and focus their efforts on trying to comfort me, regardless of what they know about my loss.

But I do not see my view as depressing, cynical, or tragic. I don't carry a heavy burden or sulk helplessly as I dream of the day when I will see her again when I, too, die. Instead, I see my transition into a full life as my greatest strength. I no longer hide behind any confusion and pain or fool myself into believing something that I cannot be sure is any more real than a dream, like I did as a child. I am now able to face the reality of her death with a peaceful heart, remembering what was so precious about her. The overwhelming love that she graced us with for the short time she was here will last a lifetime in the very fiber of my being.

This is not to say that I've never felt any grief since her death. My life has been a transition and the events that followed were not simple. We were torn, my brothers and sisters and I, torn apart by our pain and by our healing. I felt selfish when I tried to live normally. As a little girl, I was confused as to how I should go on about my life. Could I still laugh and smile? Was it okay to joke and play, or would everybody think I was cold-hearted and unaffected? It hit me hard. It hit us all hard. But I knew, then and now, that I didn't experience the worst of it. Although I was young, I could see the severe and heartbreaking effects it had on my mother. She did all she could to stand tall and shield us from emotional distress, but her own pain seemed to seep right through her skin. Still, she kept her face soft and warm, and always welcoming. She never stopped being a mother, and she knew that, even if just for us, life had to continue. For that, she is the strongest woman I know.

I am certain that I would not have witnessed my mother's true strength had my sister not passed. The respect I

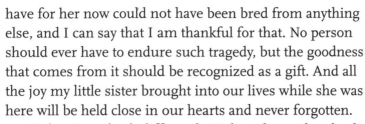

have for her now could not have been bred from anything else, and I can say that I am thankful for that. No person should ever have to endure such tragedy, but the goodness that comes from it should be recognized as a gift. And all the joy my little sister brought into our lives while she was here will be held close in our hearts and never forgotten.

Today, I see death differently. Today, I know that death doesn't overcome love. But it also doesn't transcend life. My life is better because she was a part of it, even for the two short years that she lived, and I know this is true for my family, as well. It gives me peace to know that I can live happily, converting misfortune into an immense appreciation for what I have gained from the loss. So don't feel sorry for me. Don't send me flowers or gifts or tell me that everything will be all right and I'll see her when I get to Heaven.

In *As I Lay Dying*, when William Faulkner wrote, "My mother is a fish," I immediately knew what he meant. Like a fish, my little sister was here, and now she is not. I may or may not see her again, but I don't really need to, because she lives inside of me. The love she has given me and the strength to grow and move on, the ability to see light and feel comfort in a dark and crowded space, all of this will last me until I am not here, until I am no more. She will live in my heart, but nowhere else. Still, I could never ask for more than what she has already given me.

My little sister is a fish, and I am okay with that.

Desirée attends the University of California, Berkeley. She is majoring in integrative biology with a focus in paleontology. She grew up in Riverside, California, with her parents and her six siblings, and loves spending time with her family. In her free time, she enjoys hiking, running, and playing volleyball.

The Time of Your Life

by Jaclyn Allavie

I will be the first to admit: I don't have it all figured out.
I am far from wise and my life is anything but scripted.
Describing to others the "meaning of life" when I have yet
to figure out my own existence is a little complicated. My
grand entrance into a, shall we say, less-than-booming economy, has been anything but a smooth transition. However,
there are a few things I know. I know that my worth is not
determined by my immediate post-graduation fate. I know
that I am in a place of complete spontaneity, capable of
doing just about anything I set my mind to with no need for
urgency. And I am starting to learn that this world is for living, not worrying. Each and every day, I am learning to love
myself for the individual I am becoming, but this path has
not always been easy for me.

I recently graduated from college with my bachelor's
degree—in three years. Where did the time go and why my
ever-present race against the clock? In my effort to get to the

next step in life, I sometimes forget the most important part of the equation: the experience. Often, I am reminded of a line from *The Phantom Tollbooth,* a favorite childhood book I read years ago. In it, Norton Juster wrote, "Time is a gift, given to you, given to give you the time you need, the time you need to have the time of your life." Today this means to me that life does not start tomorrow, or after my master's degree, but right now.

Upon reflection, having what I have deemed my "gap year" from schooling has been a blessing in disguise. I have had the opportunity to stop my frenetic race to the next achievement, to truly reflect on my passions and interests. The thing is, life often tumbles out in an amalgamation of odds and ends, not anything like I had been planning. And let me tell you, I am a planner! I was born to write to-do lists, categorize my closet, and calendar every last detail of my life. But as I get older, I am learning the difference between focusing attention on an important task at hand and obsessing over a problem. I have to remind myself, sometimes daily, to stop, take a deep breath, and unwind.

I do not say this lightly: I have mastered the art of worrying. I am constantly worried about the next hoop to jump through, whether it's grad school, finding a good job, or developing my personal relationships. Decisions are not the only facet of my life where I crave perfection; my quest for the ideal body image still lingers as well.

I can remember my body dissatisfaction as far back as elementary school, but it all came to an apex in high school. There was hardly a moment when I wasn't critical of how I looked, and I became completely obsessed with food, calories, and weight. Even worse, I became completely devoid of self-love. These thoughts took over my life until I had no control. It started with a simple diet that slowly, over time, morphed into a hideous monster. I weighed myself 10 times a day on the good days. Everything I did, every thought I had, was consumed by this obsession. All I wanted was to be skinny. I didn't just ignore the headaches, fatigue, and dizziness. Suddenly, they empowered me and gave me this false sense of control. I felt superior that I could go one more day without those extra calories and somehow, this eased the indescribable desire for perfection that haunted my dreams. My thoughts changed and the happiness I once had was enveloped by depression and loneliness. Everything irritated me except my focus on the number on the scale.

The best way I can describe it was that I was drowning, lost in a downward spiral that had grabbed my ankle and was pulling me to the bottom of the pool—only, I didn't want to escape. The addiction consumed my heart and mind, body and soul, and it almost felt . . . good. The irony about my obsession was that the moment I felt closest to victory with my "goal" weight was when I was reeling out of control.

Years of psychotherapy and a college education later, I am facing the difficulties involved on the road to personal recovery and body acceptance. It has not been easy and I often falter. What I can tell you is that, after years of despising my own being and wishing I was someone else, a part of me wanted out. The sliver of me that had not been destroyed by my eating disorder was crying to break free, and ultimately, I knew that nothing was as important as my health. I started to recognize when my disorder was talking and I started to have choices.

Today is so much better, and part of the healing for me has been surrounding myself with good people, friends and family who love me and support my personal growth. In my erratically disordered years, I found that my actions did nothing but push away those I loved and those who cared about me. Now I focus on the good people in my life with whom I have been blessed and understand how fortunate I am to have such amazing support. Since my negative body perception has a ripple effect on other areas of my life, I now understand that I should not burden myself with unnecessary expectations that set me up for certain internal disaster. Though I am vigilantly keeping the monster of my eating disorder at bay with a healthy lifestyle and positive self-talk, my personal struggle with my body image has not entirely abated. I work toward self-love and acceptance every day, and I am excited to embrace the woman I am becoming. There is no hurry on my road to recovery. I am certain I will get there.

Jaclyn earned a bachelor's degree in international relations from the University of California, San Diego. She is studying at Columbia University's School of Nursing in New York City, working toward becoming a nurse practitioner. Her favorite things include healthy living, travel, family game night, photography, E.E. Cummings, and contemplating life's next adventure.

To Be or Not to Be

by Ashleigh Greenstreet

A memory can stay in your life for an eternity, or it can be a flash that is gone in a moment. It can be a thought, a passing idea, or a stamp on the brain that stays imprinted on the soul. Many of the memories that visit me aren't very happy. I wish I could say that I grew up like most children, that I remember more good in my childhood than bad, but I'd be lying. I'm not saying that I didn't have wonderful moments here and there, but the bad ones haunt me and color the choices I make on a daily basis.

My memories consist of shades of darkness that rewind and play back in my mind like a black-and-white movie. I remember that darkness and a fear of the dark, a fear that stays with me even today, from not having electricity in the house for days at a time. I grew up in a home of addiction, where the choices that my parents made for our family were anything but good. And the darkest of days is a memory I can relive instantly if I choose to. It was the day my parents were taken away by a white van full of people with weapons. Everyone was screaming and there was complete chaos. My brothers and I were taken to the neighbors' house, where we waited for my parents to come back home. I don't remember how long they were gone. I just remember looking through the window, looking and waiting.

It took a little time and maturity to figure out that my parents were involved in a drug raid. The people in that white van were police officers and they were searching our home for drugs. There were so many people in and out of my house that day, and so many faces, but in my mind, everything was moving in slow motion. It was like I was stuck in a nightmare and couldn't move. Our house was completely destroyed. It looked like they had taken whole bookshelves and dresser drawers and thrown them on the floor, with papers, clothes, and our whole life scattered everywhere. And I know that day I almost became an orphan.

The police gave my parents a choice. They had to choose drugs or choose us. But my brothers and I didn't have a choice. We had to go back to our parents and hope that they made better decisions. We had to hope that at least one of them would choose us.

From that single memory, that single day, I started to pay attention to the impact of choices. I didn't want a life of drugs or barely making ends meet. I wanted a life of light, of hope, of a chance at making a future for my children that they wouldn't have to overcome.

I remember reading William Shakespeare's *Hamlet,* a play about a troubled young man. Hamlet was tormented about how to deal with a difficult family situation. He even wondered if committing suicide would be the best way to escape or if he should live with his family's choices and just make the best out of the situation. Hamlet contemplated whether it was better "to be or not to be," and I have asked myself the same question many times. Unlike Hamlet, though, I didn't struggle much with the answer. I chose life. I chose education. I chose to be my own person. When given the choice of my parents' lives or choosing a different path of my own, to go to college and not to get involved in drugs, I chose to be a student, to be a participant, to pursue my passion and love for dance. I chose not to be a high school dropout; I chose not to be a teen parent. Above all, I chose not to be someone other than myself, and my choice in pursuing my education is, above all else, to seek out knowledge and make a positive difference in the world.

I am not sorry that I was deprived of great childhood memories. I am not sorry that I am afraid of the dark, and I am not even sorry that I grew up in a home of addiction. I love my parents very much, because they humbly understand the wrongs they have done with their past decisions, and today, they choose to live a life making better choices. The past will always stay with me, but I have learned to use it as a way to keep my eyes focused on my dreams. As I continue to work toward my dream of becoming an art teacher, I pray not to be the kind of parent my children have to heal from, even though I know that difficult obstacles are certain to come my way. But more than anything, I know that today I have the choice of whether or not to be true to myself, to my convictions, and to my heart. The beauty in all this is that I choose to have choices.

Ashleigh attends Riverside Community College. She hopes to attend the University of California, Riverside, for a degree in art therapy. She recently married her high school sweetheart, and they both continue to pursue their individual dreams. Her hobbies include drawing and painting. She has also mastered babysitting and hopes to work with children in her career.

Braver than You Believe

by Vanessa Cazares

"My mom! No! I don't want to leave, I want to stay with her!" I cried, after the officers came. They had taken my little brother, my sister, and me away from our mother. It was December 28, 2005, the worst day of our lives, and it seemed as if these people did not understand this in any way. Some of the officers were in uniforms and some of them were disguised as innocent bystanders, but they were all the rudest and meanest police officers I had ever met in my life. I had never been in a kind of situation where the police intimidated me, but here they were, yelling at my little sister to sit down. Police officers were supposed to make you feel safe, right? Well, I did not feel safe at all. And since then, I have never fully regained my trust in law enforcement.

"Come with me," said the caseworker. As she said this, I had so much fear and sadness and so many other emotions going through my body. I didn't know how to react to the panic racing through me.

"We don't want to go," said my sister, but the woman didn't appear to hear us at all. She seemed like a nice person, but I desperately wanted to stay with my mother. We no longer had a choice, though. We had to go with the caseworker whether we liked it or not. This was because our mother had been involved in selling narcotics and she had lost all of her parental privileges and rights because of her bad choices.

The ride was long and silent, and I didn't know what was going to happen. As I was the oldest, I felt responsible for taking care of my brother and sister. Then the woman told us in the car that my sister and I were going to the same foster home but my brother would be going to a different one. I was shocked and outraged! I questioned her, but she had little left to say and no soothing answers for me. At that time, I had no idea what a foster home was but I couldn't bear the thought of being separated from my baby brother.

My sister and I were dropped off first at our new "home," and leaving my little brother was the hardest thing I ever had to do. He had been sound asleep in his car seat and had no idea what was happening, but he woke up as we were getting out of the car. He saw us leaving and he started to cry. This was the worst feeling ever because I couldn't hold him and I couldn't hold my pain in any longer and I started to cry. I tried to keep it together so that my little sister could see how brave I was, but it was too hard. It is still so clear in my head every time I think about it, and even today, I feel like crying when I think about the look on his face. He looked at me like he couldn't take one more person leaving him. I didn't know what to do but just cry for three days at my new home.

I was quickly enrolled at a new school. I was still sad and didn't want to do any schoolwork, but I thought about it and told myself that I needed to set a good example for my sister. I needed to try my hardest to make my dreams come true for all of us. I never thought I was going to be able to get through school, but after a while, I knew it was my only choice. I survived those next months and earned surprisingly good grades. My caseworker told me she was impressed because the children she had worked with in the past years had been too depressed to do well in school. And though the next two years that I lived in the foster home were hard for me, I needed to keep on going with my life and let go of the past if I was to ever move toward a better future. I guess it was like what A.A. Milne's Christopher Robin said when he told Winnie the Pooh, "You are braver than you believe, stronger than you seem, and smarter than you think." I found courage in my fear, strength from my pain, and resilience through my schoolwork.

My sister and I now live with my aunt, whom I have lived with for about four years. My little brother is back with us, too, and he is about to turn six. On that awful December day, he was just a baby and had his whole life in front of him, but he was alone, so I am very grateful that he came back to us. My life is pretty good today. I see my mother sometimes, too, for which I am glad as well. I often wish that things could be different and that I lived with her, because I know she loves us more than anything. She made a mistake that had devastating consequences, but I understand the mistake she made and I have forgiven her. We all are human and we all falter. I love my mother more than anyone in the world and she will always have a huge place in my heart.

Forgetting the past was not as easy as it might seem and how I view life now is very different than how I viewed it before. But it's been sort of a gift because I've gained a new belief in myself. I know I can handle just about anything, and I won't let any obstacle or challenge get in the way of accomplishing my dreams. Today I know that I am brave, that I am strong, and that I can accomplish anything if I set my mind to it.

Vanessa has grown up mostly in Riverside, California. She is now studying at the University of California, Riverside. She plans to study biology and have a career in the medical field. Vanessa was a member of the AVID program in high school and is active in the community through volunteering. She is a dedicated student and society member and a winner of an AVID scholarship.

And So...

Questions for Reflection, Discussion, and Writing

Maybe you've been told that it's the hard times that will build your character and make you a better and stronger person. Do you agree with this idea? Whether you do or do not, do you find that it doesn't always *seem* like any good will come from your struggles? The essays in this part of the book may have brought up some painful memories or touched on buried feelings about challenges you have faced. Knowing that we are not alone in our struggles and our self-discovery can bring us hope and comfort. Use these essays to help you build a bridge from one side of your pain to the other. Allow yourself to get in touch with your feelings of despair, loneliness, or fear—and also allow yourself to feel hopeful about brighter days ahead.

A single, defining moment changed *Nooreya's* life forever. What events in your life have most shaped and defined you? Reflect on the changes these events brought with them and how you feel about them now.

After *Roxana* almost died, she wrote of how she appreciated, in a new way, her ability to do seemingly ordinary tasks such as talking and swallowing. What are the activities, small or large, that you think you'd miss more than anything else, if poor health or other circumstances kept you from doing them?

Do you agree with *John* that in many instances "words are no good"? Reflect on times when words couldn't help you. Think also about times when words brought you comfort and relief, or helped you in some other way. How do you keep going when your life gets tough?

Archeé describes finding solace in volleyball after losing her mother. Are you in a sport? If so, in what ways does that sport help you mentally as well as physically? If not, what other outlets do you have for your energy and emotions, and how have these things helped you?

Kaylee believes that in some cases it's better to separate a family than to keep it together in a pattern of unhappiness, abuse, or addiction. What do you think about this? What events in your life have seemed negative to those around you but positive to you?

Krissie points out some of the things in this world that we can become addicted to or dependent on, and admits to having her own "monsters." What are your monsters? How do they keep you from living the life that you want? How can you fight these monsters?

Desirée confronts her beliefs about death after her little sister dies. What do you think happens to people after they die? Think about what might become of us when we leave this world. Do your ideas tie in directly with your religious beliefs or the beliefs of your parents or culture?

Jaclyn worries about her future choices, and also about her body image. Are there certain parts of your life that you spend a great deal of time and energy worrying about? Do you think there are any aspects of your life that you should worry about *more* than you do? How might you find a balance between thinking seriously about your future and enjoying your life in the present?

After seeing the choices her parents made, *Ashleigh* has chosen to free herself from an environment of drug abuse and to pursue her education. How much power do you think we have to choose our own paths, and how much are we shaped by our families and our circumstances? What can we learn from our poor choices and those of others?

Like Ashleigh, *Vanessa* was removed from her home due to drugs being present, but her story ended differently from Ashleigh's. Consider a tough experience you've had that revealed your own strengths to you, or showed you who you could count on. How do you think you would be different without this experience?

Part 4

Essays on Identity and Self

"I am a red balloon."

—Esperanza in Sandra Cisneros's
The House on Mango Street

A Matter of Infinite Hope

by Jimmy Kollar

It's an amazing experience seeing the realizations people make when they are put into a situation where they're no longer driven by their egos, but instead motivated to bring others closer together. Unfortunately, at the beginning of my junior year in high school, I had yet to really understand the importance of having true compassion and unity with my peers.

During my first two years of high school, I never made any real attempt to associate with most of the people who surrounded me, due to my perception of my peers and my own inflated perception of myself. My involvement and success in being part of my school's swim team made me feel as if I were separate from most of my classmates. The time I gave to this singularly competitive sport, and the success I had with it, had a negative effect on my life. Arrogance, pride, and individualism seeped into all the aspects of my life beyond the pool deck.

I truly felt that I was different from most of my peers. I associated only with people who were similar to me and I gave myself ridiculous reasons for not meeting different people. I could think someone was too smart, too stupid, too athletic, not athletic enough, or just not worthy enough for me to attempt any kind of interaction with that person. Of course, the irony in my attitude was that if someone were to meet me for the first time, he or she would be sure to judge me for a lisp I had developed while having braces on my teeth years earlier. But here I was, judging them for idiosyncrasies that were even more superficial.

Thankfully, these perceptions of life that I had at the beginning of my junior year began to change through the experiences that I had in my literature class. I enjoyed everything about this class, from the books we were studying to the class projects we were assigned, and my enthusiasm inspired me to try to really understand what I read. The literature we were asked to examine and the unique classroom discussions and projects that went along with what we were reading made it easy to relate to what was happening in my own life. As the year progressed, the literature slowly helped me recognize and address my own character defects.

The first book that had a true impact on me was *The Great Gatsby* by F. Scott Fitzgerald. This book is about an ordinary man who amassed a great amount of wealth in his pursuit to win back the woman he loved. He was unable to impress her enough because, despite having all the money that anyone could ever desire, he did not have the status and power of a man coming from a family of great wealth. As I read about him, I realized that this kind of prejudice and focus on someone's status, instead of on his talent or merit, had affected me in a similar manner. In competitive swimming, almost all of the "good" swimmers have been swimming on club teams for many years before they join their high school swim team. I was different because I started swimming my first year of high school without any experience. Ever since I joined the swim team, I felt that I was looked down upon by "club swimmers," especially once I got to the higher-level competitions.

People who had been swimming since they were young were almost a type of aristocracy when it came to the culture of swimming. I would never be one of "them." I would never have the prestige of being a "club swimmer," and I hated that feeling. As it turned out, though, I slowly began to realize that I was being treated with the same condescending arrogance that I had given to my peers in school. How hypocritical and unfair my perceptions of people were!

Reading *The Great Gatsby* helped me start to see my peers in a new light. As we moved through more novels and class projects, I saw how literature had begun to have a major impact on how I looked at the people around me. I saw how blatantly ignorant I had been in judging others. I saw with a sudden clarity that, whatever they did with their time outside of the classroom, every one of my classmates had something unique and interesting about them. For the first time, I truly made an effort to meet these people I spent my days with, and not only did I gain an incredible amount of respect for many of the people around me, but I also became good friends with several of my fellow classmates.

Fitzgerald's narrator in *The Great Gatsby* reflects on the idea that "reserving judgments is a matter of infinite hope." I feel like that's what literature has given me. Hope. Hope for myself and hope for others. How I judge other people and their individual merit has completely changed after reading these books. I understand now that people are just people: interesting, smart, funny, and kind people who are, in many ways, just like me.

Jimmy Kollar *(jim • me koe • lar) n; James, Jim* **1** *: currently attends University of California, Berkeley.* **2** *: life mainly consists of being with friends, studying, playing sports, and sleeping.* **3** *: doesn't have any sure idea on what to do in life yet, but is looking forward to the future.*

Any Way That Suits You

by Adam Fletcher

So here's the truth: I want everyone to like me. I want them to respect me, to be proud of me, and to value my accomplishments. But if I really get honest, I just want them to value who I am, with or without my accomplishments; and because I want others to like me so much, it often undermines staying true to who I am. Though those around me would probably look at my achievements and classify what I have done so far as successful, I don't think I've done nearly enough.

First and foremost, I long for the adoration and approval of my parents; I want them to be proud of me. I try to please my parents by keepings good grades, by being a musician, and by being a good kid in general, but I always seem to fall short. This is also made more difficult due to my remarkable younger sister. Often, I have sat in the shadows and watched while my sister has bested everything I have done. Though I love her, I have found it hard, sometimes, to watch her get higher grades, impress more teachers, and win countless awards, from $100 cash prizes to dance scholarships to Best in State. And every time, I see how truly proud my parents are of her. It's those rare times when I feel *I* have made them proud that are simply exhilarating to me, and I tend to extend that desire to almost anyone in my life whom I value. I live for the moments when I can put a smile on someone's face, knowing I've pleased them or made them happy. I often push myself to the brink, just for one pat on the back or a "Good job, Adam!"

But I feel crushed when I fail or disappoint anyone. I haven't only set an extraordinarily high level of expectations for myself, but I've allowed others to do so, as well. Because of this, I feel constant pressure to live up to these standards and I take it upon myself to be among the best. And that's the problem, for if I disappoint people, which I surely will, I fear they won't like me anymore, and I can't stand the thought of that happening.

In my perpetual endeavor to make people happy, I end up sacrificing my individuality and personality. I often think of *The Adventures of Huckleberry Finn* by Mark Twain. Though the entire book is about the development of Huck Finn, in the end, Huck still gives in to everything Tom wants to do, no matter the cost to Huck's integrity. He just wants to keep his friend happy with him. Huck has an attitude that I can completely relate to when he says to Tom, "Any way that suits you suits me." I believe that I have fallen prey to the exact same mindset, and constantly relinquish who I am to fit in with whoever happens to be the person I want to please. I am afraid of saying anything that may be viewed unfavorably or conflict with anyone's beliefs, so I usually end up going along with whatever is said, or I simply say nothing. It has been easier to take the road of least resistance so that people like me, yet my inner self yearns to be heard, trying to break free from the steel cage my expectations have created. Huck made me realize that the necessity of keeping others happy keeps my true thoughts imprisoned behind a mask of doubt.

On the outside, I have developed a persona as a mild-mannered, easygoing, smart guy, and I'm happy with this image—as long as others are okay with it, of course. But on the inside, I am a hopeless romantic who writes songs and watches romantic comedies. Knowing that my dad (or probably anyone else who has a certain image of me) would disapprove of this side of me, I've kept it hidden behind the typical male stereotype of a guy who watches violent movies and listens to hard rock. I am also terrible at making decisions, because if my decision ends up making someone unhappy, it takes me a very long time to forgive myself. It seems safer, therefore, to just stay quiet and let others pave the way. I have plenty of opinions and many experiences that I could share with others, but I'm afraid that being just me won't be enough. Like Huck, I keep up a facade of who I am convinced others want me to be.

But there is hope for me. As I get to know and trust myself with close friends, I am able to express my true personality more and more. As I become more confident that these friends like the *real* me, I open up and share who I really am. I can be such a different person around my close friends and my sister; I worry less about filtering my thoughts and express my honest opinions. I even show my weaknesses and open up about what I am really feeling, and day by day, it keeps getting easier.

Though at a first glance—and sometimes even at a second glance—I am not really who I am, I am finding that being open with others is changing my life. I still feel the pressure to agree with people much of the time, but I am slowly breaking out of that shell of conformity. Maybe, just maybe, if I continue to accept myself for who I am, what I like, how I think, and how I see the world, no matter who I feel I have to impress, maybe that "Good job, Adam!" won't matter so much after a while.

Adam was one of two student editors of this book. He is now an electrical engineering major at the University of California, Los Angeles. Adam plays piano, guitar, and, as part of the UCLA marching band, trombone. He and his younger sister grew up in Moreno Valley, California, and Adam appreciates his heritage from both his white father and Filipina mother. In high school, Adam served as chairperson of the Community Foundation Youth Grantmakers, and he played Danny Zuko in Grease.

Climb Into His Skin

by Priscilla Nguyen

Chatter. That's what I call it. That constant gossip that can be heard around me as I move through my day. As I sit and reflect, though, I realize that I've taken part in this chatter that I so despise. After all, I have jumped to conclusions many a time. Yet I have no right to stereotype a person or decide if I like someone or not based solely on what others tell me about him or her, or even what I see with only my eyes. While thinking about this, I remember a novel I read in my American literature class, a book called *To Kill a Mockingbird* by Harper Lee. I suddenly understand what the character Atticus meant when he said, "You never really understand a person until you consider things from his point of view . . . until you climb into his skin and walk around in it." Had those around me in high school taken the time to get to know me, they would have known what kind of person I am and they also would have known my heart. Instead, they indiscriminately wrote me off. But how many times had I done the exact same thing to others?

Throughout high school, people often told me they thought that I was demanding, snobbish, and even unfriendly based on their first impressions of me. These first impressions may have been based on quick glimpses into my personality, but certainly not much more. I am sure I lost my temper, cried in public, and laughed at the top of my lungs, for I am not a cardboard cutout with a smile pasted onto my face every second of every day. I am human. I feel every sort of emotion. I am not defined by the clothes that I wear, or the way I style my hair, or even by the activities I enjoy. These are simply the surface layers of who I am, labels pasted on me by others who have had little interaction with me. But they were just as wrong about me as I had been about others.

I was surprised how little change there was from high school patterns during my first year in college, for all around me, I heard students complain about new acquaintances and watch them form fast opinions of those around them. They would ramble on and on about something that someone had done, and then, too often, pass judgments based on first impressions, some out of envy, some from spite, and others from their own insecurities. At times, as I listened to their stories and the reasons for such ill feelings, I unconsciously began to form my own judgments about the situation. When I became aware of my opinions unfairly coming together, I questioned if there was any truth to what these people were saying, or if it was all just nonsense. I tried to stay neutral in these situations as best I could; otherwise I'd be a hypocrite. I told myself, repeatedly, that first impressions are not everything, but it was so hard to stay out of that trap of putting people into little boxes and leaving them there.

Today, I still hear a constant chatter of voices. I catch fragments of conversations of "he said" and "they did" and "I heard," and I can't seem to escape them. The whispering, the looks—they are everywhere I go. Worse, it's not just my peers, for I see this same behavior in adults and children alike, judgments that are made and passed from one person to another in a split second, stereotypes that then become so deeply rooted and embedded into everyday thinking that they are no longer conscious thoughts. It's been said that first impressions can tell a lot about a person, and that one poor decision can bring about lasting criticism and opinions. It seems to me, though, that these first encounters shouldn't be the determining factor about who a person truly is. These initial labels are false advertisements, showing only a fraction of the human soul.

Today, unlike most of my peers, I don't want to simply guess or make assumptions about who these people are that I see in my daily life. I want to move past that first impression and what I have been told and see what it's like to walk a while on their path. I try to approach every individual I encounter without an opinion and say "hello" with a smile on my face. If I get into a pickle with anyone, I no longer wish to cut them out, but instead work to see the situation from their perspective.

Today, I strive to live out my life with Lee's words in my heart. As I sit here at the end of my first year of college, I can grasp a better understanding of what Lee meant in her writing. I am on my own in a different environment and am no longer surrounded by teachers and friends who have come to know me well. As I wake up each day, I remind myself that everyone has a story. We are all different in our own ways, yet we are so similar. I can get to know someone only by looking past what is merely visible to my naked eye. I don't know what a person has gone through; I can only surmise from what I see and hear, but I know that there must be much more to their stories. By climbing into their worlds and experiencing their journeys, a better sense of appreciation for them is inevitable, and the things they treasure deep in their hearts will become clear to me. No more assumptions . . . just a lot of climbing inside and walking around these days.

Priscilla is currently studying economics at the University of California, Irvine. She grew up in Orange County with her parents and four sisters until she was 12, when the family relocated to Riverside. In her free time, Priscilla enjoys being with friends and family, as well as playing volleyball, hiking, reading, listening to music, and being outdoors.

Different Drummer

by Cory Scott

Let me share with you how literature has been with me
from the beginning of my academic career. During a parent-
teacher conference with my first-grade teacher, Mrs. Dorsey,
my parents suggested that I was doing poorly in school
because I "marched to the beat of a different drummer."
Mrs. Dorsey's calm response was, "Cory doesn't march to
the beat of a different drummer. He hears the same drums
as everyone else but he chooses not to march."

When I was brainstorming about what piece of literature most spoke to me, I have to admit that I was stuck,
and to be honest, that surprised me; after all, I had always
been a prodigious reader. I was sure that I could think of
some memorable quotes quite easily, but thinking of a
quote wasn't the problem; the problem was finding one
that was actually applicable. I considered using one of the
better puns from *Hamlet*, because I like puns and I think
my sense of humor is a good demonstration of who I am.

134

A quote from *Crime and Punishment* would make me seem intelligent and mysterious. If I used dialogue from *The Grapes of Wrath* I could capture some of Steinbeck's prose. But these are more about what I think, not who I am. It was at this point that I realized how the words my parents and Mrs. Dorsey borrowed from Thoreau's *Walden* were a gift, a gift I would carry safely with me, to take out and look at whenever being different became difficult.

Thoreau's words remind me of the controversy surrounding the works of Euclid, a Greek mathematician who established a wide variety of mathematical techniques and theorems. *The Elements* is a compilation of Euclid's work, and it begins with five postulates, upon which all of his other ideas stand. A postulate is a mathematical idea that we assume to be true. If all of mathematics is a house, then theorems are the bricks, and postulates are the clay that makes up those bricks.

Almost immediately after Euclid published *The Elements*, there was controversy over poor number four; some people believed it, some didn't, and most thought it shouldn't be considered a postulate at all. This divergence resulted in many, many attempts over the years to prove the fourth postulate. Some of these proofs are straightforward and some of them are not, but they all have one thing in common: none of them worked. No one was ever successful in proving this postulate. However, through these attempts, a new area of mathematics was discovered: non-Euclidean geometry, in which Euclid's fourth postulate does not hold true. This kind of geometry follows an entirely different set of rules than the kind that is taught in high school.

Non-Euclidean geometry has always fascinated me. Like men walking to a different beat, the mathematicians involved in developing this branch of study were harshly ridiculed by their peers. It was not until relatively recently that the mathematical community accepted non-Euclidean geometry as valid. As long as I have known the saga of these mathematicians and their work, I have admired them and their willingness to be different in the face of disapproval.

The idea of being different is essential to my individual philosophy. Mind you, I'm not talking about rejecting things out of hand simply because they're popular, or being different for difference's sake. Instead, I believe, like all the other non-Euclidean mathematicians, that I should be different when being different has merit. Being different could result in dressing differently, or reading nonstop for pleasure's sake, or having a Tinfoil Hat Day—which is March 26, by the way—with friends. The specifics don't really matter. Be spontaneous, or predictable. Be a conformist, or don't. March to the same beat as everyone else, or your own, or none at all. After all, as Thoreau noted over a century ago, "If a man does not keep pace with his companions, perhaps it is because he hears a different drummer. Let him step to the music which he hears, however measured or far away."

Cory is an amateur logician who graduated as salutatorian and received an International Baccalaureate diploma. In between proving theorems and nurturing a fledgling software company, he drinks too much coffee, reads, and listens to swing music. He attends Colorado College and is currently studying logic and set theory abroad in Budapest, Hungary. He aspires to be a mad scientist someday.

Place by the Window

by AJ Almaguer

I will never forget the moment when my mother found out that I was gay. My most vivid memory is of her eyes while she yelled at me. Her eyes weren't those of disappointment. Oh, no; she looked at me with eyes of hatred, shame, confusion, and disgust. She looked at me with frustration that her God-given son was not the "perfect little boy" that she had raised. She asked what she did wrong. She told me that I was going to hell. She threatened to kick me out. But she couldn't do anything about this. I was still her son.

I always feared this conversation that I knew I would eventually have with my parents. It isn't fair that anyone has to grow up ashamed of his or her sexuality. It isn't fair that my parents not only have to accept their son's partner, but also have to accept that his partner is a man. But as unfair as these things are, I believe that my sexuality has actually been a blessing. Dealing with my parents' homophobia has given me the motivation and strength to be the successful man that I am today.

Growing up, it never occurred to me that I could be gay. My parents always said it was wrong, taboo, so naturally, I didn't think that I would be one of "them." I dated a girl in high school and that ended quickly—we didn't click. Then I met my first boyfriend. At first we were just friends, but as we developed a deep attachment for each other, it was becoming clearer that it was something much more than friendship, and, frankly, it surprised us both.

Unfortunately, I had the agony of facing all this after my mom got on my computer and read my emails. I knew she was suspicious of my relationship, but our discretion and her denial had greatly helped the facade. My mom forced me to break up with my boyfriend when she found out, but I knew deep down that what I had with him was good and that it made me happy.

I had hoped that my mother would find out about my sexuality because I sat down and talked to her and my dad. But it didn't happen that way. I couldn't face them. I needed time to go off to college, build my identity, gather some courage, and understand that I'm not broken . . . I'm just gay. I realized that I would be setting myself up for failure if I were not strong enough to embrace my own identity. I prayed that I could learn to love myself for all that I am: gay, bi, straight, whatever, and that my parents would come to accept and love me for who I am, because no matter what, I was still their son.

I was starting to see that the most important thing I needed to do was to learn to love myself for who I was becoming and just try to live my life. I tried not to berate myself with all the confusing questions of sexuality and religion; after all, the Bible is up for interpretation and from what I've gathered, people have used it to justify some pretty nasty acts in this world. Now, I'll admit: I'm not super religious, but my mother is. Instead of worrying about how she might pass judgment, however, I decided to leave the judgment up to the Big Man.

It was this understanding of my own feelings that helped me stand up to my mother after I went to college 400 miles from home. The distance allowed me to form my own identity, though during my first year in college I continued to question my sexuality. I even dated another girl to see how it felt. I told her from the start that I'd been with a man in the past. She respected that and it didn't bother her, but after a couple months of dating, I knew that staying with her would be unfair to both of us. It was time to explore my sexuality further. But gay or straight, I wasn't about to hook up with random people. If there was ever a time that I supported celibacy, it was during this time. I learned that I would figure out my sexuality much more easily this way and with much less heartache. Sex makes things complicated and things are already complicated enough.

A quote from *The House on Mango Street* gave me direction while I was trying to figure out my identity. Esperanza recalled an image of her great-grandmother many times, and it created the idea that the women on Mango Street were imprisoned, not by their houses, but by their lives and the beliefs they had about their lives. She remembered how her great-grandmother "looked out the window her whole life, the way so many women sit their sadness on an elbow. . . . I have inherited her name, but I don't want to inherit her place by the window." They were stuck because of their husbands, family situations, and lack of opportunity, but more importantly, they were stuck because of their beliefs about themselves, many times beliefs that others placed on them. Like Esperanza, I knew that was not how I was willing to live my life, and like Esperanza, I believe those women could have done more to escape their prisons and take charge of their own destiny. So that's what I did. I left home for college, figured out what I loved to do, and created an identity for myself.

So here's the confession: I still need to have that complete conversation with my mother and other family members about being gay. I'm not sure when I will have the talk, but at least I know that I'm ready to do it on my own terms now. I have a strong sense of who I am. I opened myself to new beliefs, new thoughts, and new people. I know for sure what my sexuality is. I know for a fact that there isn't anything wrong with me. I love who I am. I am an educated queer man of color, and I am still my mother's son.

AJ spent 10 years becoming a classically trained pianist but stopped playing after heading to college to explore other interests. In addition to studying engineering at the University of California, Berkeley, he became a swing dance instructor and founded Berkeley Engineers and Mentors (BEAM), one of the largest mentoring organizations on campus. He is the first in his family to graduate from college, receiving bachelor's degrees in mechanical engineering and materials science engineering.

When the Light Turns Blue

by *Ricky Dama*

We can all remember back to a time in our childhoods when the world was a simple and wondrous place, when nothing needed explaining and we just saw things as they were. As I get older, though, I find that I lack the ability to see the world so clearly and realize that perhaps ignorance really is bliss. As a kid, I read Shel Silverstein's *A Light in the Attic* again and again. Over the years, one poem, "Signals," stood out and stayed with me like a familiar nursery rhyme:

> When the light turns green, you go.
> When the light turns red, you stop.
> But what do you do when the light turns blue
> With orange and lavender spots?

As a child, I only took his words for face value, and so I frequently spent my time in the car looking for this ever-elusive multicolored light. Now, of course, I see the real point of his playful words. The message beneath the simple rhyme strikes me deeply. All too often, we are faced with questions that have no obvious answers.

My whole life, when I came to one of these lights, I simply stopped, not knowing which way to go. I felt terrible pressure from those behind me, honking and yelling, telling me to go or turn, or just do something; but I was never sure where I really wanted to go or what direction I wanted to take, so I'd sit, frozen. After all, did the bugs that flew into my windshield plan on ending up there? What was the best way to turn? What was the best road to take? To be honest, I've had many different dreams for my future and have worked toward each one, but I feel as if I'm just going in circles.

In first grade, I was content with whatever I did. I played soccer and chased girls, not caring that I was never really any good at either. By the fourth grade, though, I desperately wanted to be popular, so I made pitiful attempts to imitate pop culture and pretended to be "cool." This meant sacrificing many parts of me that I thought made up who I was, from the way I dressed to the music I listened to. I was willing to change it all for a ticket to the top. When it came time to go to high school, I'd grown tired of pretending and having nothing to show for it. So I chose to turn at the light, taking the strange and multihued signal as a chance for a new direction. I transferred to a new school and focused on academics.

I was happy to finally be myself and not care about what others thought of me. The classes I took and the clubs I joined were fun, and the people I met were amazing. I joined a sport for the first time and surprised others, but especially myself, when I chose wrestling. No one had ever pegged me for the type to do a contact sport. It turned out that I wasn't half bad at wrestling and made a name for myself. This made me happy because I felt like I was finally doing something that fit me and not something that fit the image of what anyone else expected of me. But my self-acceptance was short-lived. I started joining clubs just to be in them and taking classes I didn't like because I felt pressured to keep up with others. Eventually, I became just as fake as I'd ever been. The only difference was that now I justified my decisions with the prospect of a "better future."

I was disgusted with myself after I realized this. Here I was, already working on the future, yet right back where I started in the first place. It turned out that I was going in a big circle after all. So what happened at that signal light? Apparently, it seemed I could only be happy once I was able to tell myself to shut up when it came to internal doubts— and perhaps tell others to quiet down a bit, too, when it came to external doubts. Popularity, respect, and intelligence are all worth a small nod of acknowledgment, but I won't ever be happy unless I accept myself for who I am.

In the past, when I came to a blue light, I just drove straight through to satisfy people. Now, I think the most important thing in life is being able to roll down the window and tell those people to mind their own business. I won't tell you what to do when you get to one of these lights, and I hope you don't mind if I don't always care what you think I should do, either. Because you're the only one who has to live with your decision about which direction you're going to take. Today, I'm willing to live with my own decision, too. So buckle up, enjoy the ride, and try finding your own way.

Ricky attends Pomona College after graduating from high school as co-valedictorian. Ricky's goals in life include work in environmental science or whatever the universe lays out for him, although he's inclined to think it will probably involve some type of math or science. He is participating on his school dance team and his favorite class is Rock and Roll History.

Majority Rule

by Paul Gierz

As I was first entering my teenage years, my father sat down
and attempted to explain the nature of the world to me. I
suppose this is a natural instinct for a parent. I cannot really
say that he did a particularly wonderful job of it, for as a
mathematician, he's not a very eloquent man. My father told
me that a smart man thinks with his head. My mother, casually listening in on our male-bonding conversation, called
out from across the kitchen that a brave man thinks with his
heart. Thinking back, this is not a very complex philosophy,
but it had enormous implications for me once I left home.
Though it was my father's words I was focusing on at the
time, it was a combination of his view and my mother's that
I have tried to live by ever since.

Now, there is a clear distinction between an individual's
sense of right and wrong and what might be socially considered to be just and unjust, but I don't believe this distinction

comprises the entire moral dilemma. It seems that we spend more time wondering if our choices are the ones we wish to have rather than thinking about choices we actually have. While I am in no way an expert, I have picked up a thing or two along the way, and it seems to me that, whether we like it or not, the majority of our choices in the end revolve around finding happy and successful relationships. I probably don't need to speculate on exactly how difficult this can be, but personal principles have been important for me in dealing with my choices.

The difficulty for me has been mostly in the way others seemed to shun this whole concept. The increasing tendency to overlook the basic social etiquette we were taught as children has made it difficult to interact successfully as adults. When my father told me to think with my head, it seemed he was telling me to stick to my principles and my upbringing rather than allow myself to be carried away by the flood of what my grandfather would scornfully call "uncivilized youth." On the other hand, I interpreted my mother's statement as recommending an altruistic approach to life. It would verge on arrogance for me to say that I have always followed that advice, but I can say that I have tried to be helpful and available to my friends whenever they needed me. These days, however, I am more frequently reminded of the words of advice another father gave his son. In Harper Lee's *To Kill a Mockingbird*, Atticus Finch has a heart-to-heart discussion with his son about the inappropriate and immoral behavior of some of the people in town. Atticus tells his son that the "one thing that doesn't abide by majority rule is a person's conscience." These words ring true for me, and I can easily recall my own father's words from the recesses of my mind.

Not surprisingly, my decision to listen to my conscience has not always been met with a particularly enthusiastic spirit. I am often faced with the other side, seeing many of my peers taking the easy way out. More and more people seem to view the choices presented to them in a fairly selfish manner. They attempt to maximize their own benefits while perhaps not entirely ignoring others, but certainly expending a minimum amount of thought on them.

While my own solution may not be particularly elegant or effective, I believe it is the right thing to do. I will continue to stick to the ethics and ideals that I was taught growing up. I say this in spite of the fact that genuine forms of friendliness and kindness require more and more bravery from me as the years go by, something I think my mother might refer to as having more heart. And while my ideals may not be mirrored by others, at least—as Harper Lee put far more elegantly than I could—my conscience will be clear.

Paul is currently studying environmental science at the University of Frankfurt in Germany. Paul enjoys playing music, rock climbing, and sailing. He also likes taking up space in cafés while sipping on coffee, perusing a newspaper, and dabbling in philosophy. Paul recommends reading while listening to good music as an excellent escape.

Beautiful Fool

by Kelly Nielsen

Everything is terrible. Nothing makes sense anymore; the
world is crashing down around me and I seem to be the
only one who can feel the shaking. I may not have been
everywhere, but I *feel* like I have seen everything and done
everything. I have found myself in situations that I did not
belong in, that I should never have been in. More importantly, I've found myself in situations that have given me the
chance to learn something of value, as well as the ability to
grow and mature as a person.

I'm 20 years old and I have lived in Riverside,
California, my entire life. I know every inch of this place
and it is becoming smaller and smaller by the day. Everyone
knows everyone; everyone has dated someone who knows
someone who is related to someone's best friend or cousin
whom I know. There are no secrets here; there is no place
to hide and no one to confide in with complete and total
security. I can see the air I breathe, but there is nothing

fresh, nothing but meaningless chatter filling my lungs. It's suffocating. I'm beginning to feel as if I have worn out this place. It has my footprints, my mistakes, my broken heart, my laughter, and my life painted around it in every shade imaginable. In *The Great Gatsby*, F. Scott Fitzgerald's Daisy says to her cousin, "I think everything's terrible anyhow. . . . And I know. I've been everywhere and seen everything and done everything." When I read that, it was as if she was speaking my heart aloud.

When my parents divorced and my mother started her new life, I chose not to be a part of it. I knew I wouldn't fit in. So it became just the four of us: three girls, one man, and a broken life. I watched my dad go through and pick up all the pieces and move forward, raising us the best way he knew how. My mother chose a life that I still, to this day, don't understand, and though it pains me to think maybe we weren't enough to make her stay, I also respect her courage to take her own path and do what she needed to do.

And despite the things I've been through, I am a believer. I have always believed in the best of people, even when others begged me not to. I have always believed that love will one day find me. Maybe I'm wrong, but I live with great fervor, believing that it is possible to get what I really want out of life. The crazy thing is that sometimes I don't even know what I want. Sometimes I wonder if it has more to do with what I think I deserve. I don't know if I deserve to fall in love. I don't know if I deserve to have a happy family or be a successful author or wake up every day feeling happy and good about myself. But I believe I just might.

One thing is certain. I know what I don't want. I know I do not want to be like Daisy, a woman who thinks, "The best thing a girl can be in this world is a beautiful fool." I know I do not want to live my life full of regrets. I do not want to be a girl who is talked into living a life that someone else chose for her. I know I want to be a strong, independent woman, living with the hope and faith that I will one day achieve a life by my own design, with my own dreams and my own reality—a life of my own choosing.

Kelly has found where she needs to be right now, working for some of the most intellectual, fiercely kind lawyers that she's ever had the pleasure of meeting. She has also enjoyed watching her family grow closer. Her friends are her life and heart. Kelly attends Riverside Community College, focusing on literature and creative writing, and she plans to transfer to the University of California, Riverside. She is living life to the fullest and is grateful.

Shine Like Stars

by Hsuanwei Fan

It came to me in a dream as vivid as bursting fireworks, as vivid as a cloud of buzzing dragonflies and golden blossoms. A cascade of truths and realizations suddenly splashed across my mind before I awoke to a rich, velvet darkness, and the dream's discoveries settled into my heart, bringing a deep peace.

You see, I have often pondered the complexity of human identity and the interconnectedness between you, me, her, him, and them. In the moment before I surrender my full consciousness to sleep, I am many times captivated by thoughts of what makes humans the same and what makes us so different. Down to the molecular structure of our amino acids and to the atoms that make up every one of us, we are indisputably connected not only to our fellow humans, but also to all other organisms and forces in this world: the trees whose roots reach deep into the soil, the

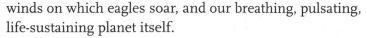

winds on which eagles soar, and our breathing, pulsating, life-sustaining planet itself.

But it's not so clear to me that others feel the same. I watch many of my altogether decent and otherwise respectable friends categorize and label people. It is incomprehensible to me how anyone could possibly conclude that any one type of distinction could indicate a person's true nature. The same color of blood flows through our veins, despite the difference in the color of our eyes, hair, and skin. Regardless of our ethnic background, something inside us is awakened by beautiful music or a bold piece of art. Yet we can be so different. One can be a huge supporter of immigration reform but be strongly opposed to abortion. A person may be attracted to people who identify as females, regardless of their physical traits, yet another person can be predisposed to fall in love only with people of a particular gender and a particular sexual identity.

It seems like most labels—even those that supposedly reflect a range of identities—are wearing thin. Labels are becoming less and less applicable in pinpointing someone's identity; slowly, people are realizing the liberty of a constantly growing spectrum of possibilities with which a person can identify. For example, for people who embrace ideas of being "gender queer" or "post-gender," labels like "homosexual" or "heterosexual" are no longer accurate. These individuals choose to be undefined and unconfined to a traditional concept of gender.

That is what flooded into my dreams that night: a burst of colorful pigments putting on a show in the IMAX stadium of my brain. Just as the previous generation responded to an older world of absolute black and white by opening people's eyes to the gray areas, I have realized that even these shades of gray no longer suffice. Instead, I now see humans, individually unique and beautiful in their own ways, as specks of pigment making up the beautiful rainbow that is the full color spectrum with its endless possibilities. Two colors may seem to be alike at first, but essentially they are unique. And when different people interact, their talents and characters come together to create something that is unique to them, just like the countless variety of hues that can be made by mixing colors.

It's on this ordinary yet spectacular day that I appreciate just how unique everyone is, and yet how each and every single one of us contributes to humanity as a whole, like strands in a beautiful tapestry telling tales of struggle and triumph. I cannot help but think of each of us as a tiny speckle of light, as if we are stars viewed from a great distance away, striving to shine our color as brightly as possible to make this world a better place. Apostle Paul, one of my favorite authors in the Bible, encourages us to "become blameless and pure, children of God without fault in a crooked and depraved generation, in which you shine like stars in the universe." So, let us shine like stars in the universe, each more brilliant than the next, and take away nothing from the world except darkness.

Hsuanwei is a Taiwanese immigrant who began learning English and the value of open-minded thinking at the age of 10. He attends Pomona College in Claremont, California. Hsuanwei is a lover of food, an art fanatic, an ardent environmentalist, an unrelenting utopian, an insatiable socialite, an aspiring Renaissance man, and a self-proclaimed idealist. He believes, more than anything, in the power of humanity to overcome obstacles.

I Am a Red Balloon

by Derek Ignatius

Now and then, I try to imagine that I can fit my whole life inside a balloon. My experiences, past, school, work, preoccupations, laptop, friends, and goals; I try to fit everything in there. Then I release it. I let my life go, stand back, and watch what happens.

When I imagined this balloon carrying my life a few years ago, I remember watching it sink, slowly but surely, straight down to my feet. My life was burdened with changes and transitions at home, and I was laden with questions of self-doubt. As a child, I always had this weird ability to adapt. I could fit in with any group of people I hung around. My whole demeanor could change in an instant depending on who I was with. I could fit in anywhere. I could be like anyone. I had a thousand identities. I was so worried about being what everyone else wanted that I never got a chance to think about what I wanted to be. I moved through life with this immense weight on my shoulders, living up to expectations and perceptions set by others. Life and its changes, though, did not sit well with me.

I now see progression as one of the beauties of life. The ability to move forward from one stage to another is a remarkable facet that we are privileged to experience; however, this was not always how I saw it. I have realized that sometimes I am so focused on who I want to be in the future that I never really stop to figure out who I am today. How can I move on and continue to the next step if I never really know what step I am standing on in the first place?

I am tied down by the worries of my future. The rush of the world around me makes it almost impossible to take the time necessary to live by my own self-government. Society has me caught up in this never-ending rat race to pursue happiness and success, but the more I try to streamline through life, the easier it becomes to push things aside, and the easier it becomes to simply stuff more and more pieces into the balloon without thinking twice about the consequences. It's when I do this that I fail to understand the separate pieces of life that define my very being. It's almost like the things inside my balloon are holding me from flight. Like Esperanza says in *The House on Mango Street,* "I am a red balloon, a balloon tied to an anchor."

It boils down to this: I have to know myself. Know who I am and what I am about. Know what makes me smile, what makes me *genuinely* smile. Know what makes me feel warm. Know my talents and know my strengths. Know what I love. I believe that I have to know my own limits and my own story in order to progress in life. If I don't know the significance of everything in my balloon when it leaves my hand, how am I going to know what I am letting go of? Would you have the confidence to let your life go, up to the mercy of the winds, without even knowing your story?

I am finding myself. I am slowly building the chapters of my story and sorting out what I love in life. Today, I embrace what I love. I embrace what makes me happy. And I am beginning to realize what is actually important to me and to my life. I am beginning to see what sets me free, what makes my life soar. I am coming to understand who I am and who I have grown to be. But I'm still weighed down, and until I'm ready, until I can release the unnecessary parts of my life that are holding me down, I remain tied to the weight of that anchor. Every now and again, I still ask myself, "What will set me free?" And so I ask you now, "What sets you free?"

Derek is an undergraduate at the University of California, Berkeley, pursuing a bachelor of science in mechanical engineering. Originally from Moreno Valley, California, he loves maintaining an active lifestyle and adventuring outdoors. Derek enjoys playing soccer and volleyball, listening to music, and having a good time with friends and family. He constantly strives to live a positive, humorous, and upbeat life.

And So...

Questions for Reflection, Discussion, and Writing

Right now, you're in the process of writing your own life story—of discovering who you are. With each new challenge, opportunity, success, and loss you experience, you add a new chapter. And while you will continue crafting this tale for the rest of your life, the chapters you compose as a teenager are especially important in discovering your identity. The essay writers in this section examined the creation of their life stories, their identities, and their values. As you look at the questions that follow, consider the similarities you have with these writers, as well as the ways in which you are unique. What is *your* story?

Jimmy describes his experience of feeling uncertain about his status in a group, and judging others in part because of this uncertainty. How easy or difficult is it for you to join new groups? What are your own experiences with judgment about your peers, and how does this influence how you interact with them? Have you ever rejected someone or been rejected because of preconceived notions—accurate or otherwise?

Adam shares his deep need to be accepted—by his parents, his friends, and even by himself. How often do you do something to please or impress others rather than staying true to yourself? How accepting are you of your own strengths and flaws?

Priscilla explores the habit many of us have of judging others based on hearsay or first impressions rather than learning who they are on a deeper level. Why do you think people tend to do this? What are some of the most common disparaging comments people say about each other, in gossip, online bullying, or cliques? How easy or difficult is it to defuse gossip and rumors once they start?

Like *Cory,* sometimes you might feel as though you hear a "different drummer" than others. Maybe you're not part of the mainstream in your school. If you relate to this description, how has that affected your overall experience? Even if you don't feel this way, think about your own identity and path. What does your "drummer" sound like? What quotes, songs, or colors would you use to represent yourself and your personality?

Have you ever, like *AJ,* hidden a part of your true self or pretended to be someone you're not because you were afraid of what others might think of you? How did that feel? How can that divide between you and others be bridged? When do you think it's worth taking a risk and being truthful about yourself even if it might change your relationships with others?

Ricky discusses the frustration that can come with trying to follow someone else's path. Write about a situation in which you were pushed to take a direction that was not of your choosing. Explain how you feel when you aren't in control of a situation, or when you feel you don't meet the expectations that are set for you.

Paul recalls the differing words of advice that he received from his father and mother. What advice—whether from parents, teachers, friends, or others—has been helpful to you in your life? As you discover more about yourself, how has your view of this advice evolved?

Kelly writes that she doesn't want to be a "beautiful fool." Instead, she wants to lead a "life of her own choosing," and to follow a path that no one dictates for her. Reflect on the differences and similarities of society's expectations and views of men and women today. Consider how you see yourself and your gender in this world. Are there social norms that you feel limited by, or do you feel free to live as you choose?

Hsuanwei addresses the way we often categorize people based on their gender, sexuality, politics, and other labels. Have you ever boxed someone into a category based on knowing just one aspect of their identity, such as sexual preference or political views? Did you change your mind about that person once you got to know him or her better? Reflect on this experience. How do you see yourself in terms of your own "categories"? Are you able to be friends with others who don't share your "category"?

Derek acknowledges the value of knowing oneself, including one's talents and limits. In an ever-changing world, it can be difficult not only to know yourself, but also to stay true to that knowledge. Take time to think about how you view yourself. What makes you genuinely smile? What are your strengths and what are your limitations? What is your story? And what sets you free?

Part 5

Essays on Goals, Dreams, and the Future

"And did you dream of anything?"
—Bernard in Aldous Huxley's *Brave New World*

Watcher of the Skies

by Quentin Burns

The first book I ever fell in love with was *Spindle's End* by Robin McKinley. When I read it now it seems simple: the world it presents is comfortable and self-contained and powerfully familiar. But reading it that first time was entirely different. It seemed ridiculously complex, and I kept getting lost in it. The images it constructed in my mind were always misty and far-off and fantastic. That's how fairy tales work, I think; they tell you that things that shouldn't talk do talk, and that people accept what they shouldn't accept and question what real people never question. But pretty soon, they're a part of you, and you forget that they didn't make sense because somehow, now, they do.

After that I went crazy. I read all of McKinley's books at a pace I'm sure I couldn't match today, and then I read what seemed like every other fairy tale and fairy tale retelling in the world. And so, upon finishing high school, I picked a university and a subject of study as reminiscent of fairyland as possible and off I went to Scotland.

So here I am, in a new land with an age-old history, and I've been living here in a way I haven't lived in Bookville since the fifth grade. I have been re-immersed in reading. The first thing they asked me to do here is read *Wuthering Heights*. It isn't the first time I've read it. The first time I read it was to annoy my mother. Actually, a lot of my literary choices have followed this pattern, but that's a sorry thing to admit, so I'm keeping it a secret.

Actually, my mother said I ought to read *Jane Eyre*, so I did. I liked the first third, was bored by the second third, and then had to give up. It was the first time in a long time that I had not finished a book, and I was distressed. I expected someone to call me out; any minute the book police were going to wander up and take away my reading license because clearly I no longer deserved it. I admit that I've tried earnestly to read it a dozen times since then, and to my chagrin, I still haven't managed to finish it even once.

Thus, reading *Wuthering Heights* was an act of rebellion. My mother always spoke of it as the Other Brontë Book, and she said that most readers were either *Jane Eyre* People or *Wuthering Heights* People, and never the twain shall meet. She took particular care to impress upon me her status as a *Jane Eyre* Person. Since we were opposites, I went into *Wuthering Heights* expecting to like it and I did. I liked it much better than *Jane Eyre,* and reporting this to my mother gave me an evil kind of satisfaction, even though she was disappointingly happy to accept my status as a *Wuthering Heights* Person. But I actually didn't *love* the book. I didn't connect with it the way my mother connected with *Jane Eyre*. I guessed this was because she basically *was* Jane Eyre, and I wasn't anyone from *Wuthering Heights*, which was a good thing because if I had been, I would have had much bigger problems than worries over what books to like or what book defined me.

But rereading the book here in Scotland was amazing— so different from the previous times. So what had changed? I went looking for someone to answer that question for me, and about the 10th place I looked was the Fat Book of Things Someone Decided I Needed to Read—actually titled the *Penguin Book of English Verse*—which is an excellent text roughly the size and weight of two bricks. In the *Book*, John Keats describes reading as a kind of exploration in his poem "On First Looking into Chapman's Homer": "Then felt I like some watcher of the skies / When a new planet swims into his ken."

My attitude toward reading and travel have both done a lot to define who I am and who I want to be, but I don't think I can say one is more profound than the other, since what I look for in books and in adventures isn't profound-ness at all. But reading Keats's poem did give me an idea about the *Wuthering Heights* question: namely, that the difference between my past and present reading of it was a difference of location, and that reading and places are, to me, critically linked.

Reading *Wuthering Heights* in Southern California's hot, taupe landscape is nothing like reading it in a small, creaky room by a cliff in a town in Scotland, where all the walls have green things growing on them and the sea is a deep gray and the horizon looks like the end of the world. The actual setting of the story is just over an hour away by train, and when I ride through that part of the country, I can understand the loneliness of the book in a totally different way than how I understood it when I lived with the back-drop of an arid desert, and where the end of the world was not the sea but a jagged line of mountains. Because I'm a foreigner, I'm romanticizing this northern sort of loneliness much more than I ever even thought about the Californian sort, and the romanticism slips easily into my reading of the book itself, as do all of a hundred little differences in my ways of relating to the two worlds.

That's nice, you say, but what is actually my point? Since reading *Spindle's End*, my main goal in life has been to read as many good books as is humanly possible. A few years ago, I added another goal: to explore as many interesting places as is humanly possible. Now I'm realizing that the two are kind of the same thing. I want to read *Wuthering Heights* in other more lonely places than this, and I want to find new books in new cities, which afterward will always remind me of the first place I found them.

I also want to tell people about the places I go and the things I read. That's actually somewhat alarming news, because I've always thought it would be excellent to be invisible. I wouldn't need to buy things, so work and school would become purely-for-fun activities. I could get on trains whenever I wanted and get off in crazy places and do crazy things and just go on like that indefinitely. Yet it seems that if there weren't a single person who knew what I was doing, it wouldn't be any fun. I love the part that comes after an adventure, the part where I get to go on and on about what I've seen and how worldly and fabulous I am.

Maybe I'd only enjoy invisibility with an audience, which sounds like a serious case of Missing the Point. Or, maybe, it sounds like being a writer.

Quentin was an International Baccalaureate recipient in high school, and she is currently an undergraduate at the University of St. Andrews in Scotland. Her favorite things include trains, tea, and cheesy science-fiction television. She hopes one day to be a famous eccentric who lives in a castle. And, perhaps, a writer.

The Lost Game

by Hongyu Chen

From a very young age, while many of my friends still had
a great passion for action figures, sharks, dinosaurs, and
paper airplanes, I was consumed by chess, a board game
perceived by many to be as boring and academic as doing
homework. Almost daily, my mother and I would hold
hands and walk together to a local chess club, where I would
spend hours shifting chess pieces around and occasionally
slamming them on the table when I found a particularly
good move. At that time, chess was not just a board game
but rather a kind of metaphor for life, with struggles, competition, hidden blessings, and unexpected misfortunes.

   After years of practice, I became very adept at chess,
participating in every tournament I could find and making
a name for myself. I came to think that I could become a
chess machine, and follow in the footsteps of the Cuban
chess legend José Raúl Capablanca, a man who lost a game

only on the rarest of occasions. But as Capablanca commented in his autobiography, *My Chess Career,* "There have been many times in my life when I came very near thinking that I could not lose even a single game. Then I would be beaten, and the lost game would bring me back from dreamland to earth." I didn't heed Capablanca's wise words. Instead, I developed an arrogance. I came to believe that, even before a game began, as long as I was sitting on one side of the board, the other side was bound to lose.

As I approached middle school, however, more of my time was directed toward my academics, and, in addition to fiercer competition, I found myself falling behind in chess. As I began to lose, first only occasionally and then almost every other game, I began to question the countless hours that I had invested. On February 12, 2006, I quit playing chess competitively altogether.

In short, competition had destroyed my passion for this game that I had once loved. Winning had made me lose sight of why I played chess in the first place, for the friends I would see, the fun and thrill of the game, and the life connections I made while playing. Instead of playing because I passionately enjoyed the game, I played to win. I felt I could not live with disappointing my parents, and my friends, but most importantly, myself. My competitive nature caused every loss to be etched into my brain as a reminder of my weakness. Ultimately, this led to one of the biggest regrets of my life.

Today, I occasionally play chess to impress a friend or pass the time, but not with the same passion and fire that I had when I was younger. I look at my childhood chess friends, the ones whom I could easily defeat six or seven years ago, who are now far beyond my playing ability. It saddens me, not because they make me feel weak or inadequate, but because they remind me of what I could have become had I not given in to my arrogance, my pride, that terrible shame that made me quit.

Throughout my life, I have always wanted to be good at things. I have wanted to achieve good grades, play the piano competitively, solve math equations with the speed of a calculator, and design intricate computer programs, all of which demand long-term effort and persistence. From time to time, however, my reality falls far short of my romanticized expectations, snapping me out of my dreams and keeping me grounded.

Because of my experience with chess, because of this great loss, I will always remember to set my competitiveness aside and push forward with my endeavors regardless of the circumstance or outcome. I hope to live so that, in the future, I will never look back at my actions with regret for everything that I could have had if I hadn't needed so badly to have it all.

Hongyu is currently a student at Dartmouth College, after graduating from high school as a co-valedictorian. In high school, he spent countless hours serving as president of the chess club both at North High School and at the University of California, Riverside. Though he no longer plays competitively, Hongyu enjoys teaching young children how to play chess, because it reminds him of his own childhood. In his free time, Hongyu loves spending time outdoors, computer programming, and playing the piano.

Missions Are Stupid

by Sushana Ullah

In his novel *The Unbearable Lightness of Being*, Milan Kundera wrote, "Missions are stupid. . . . I have no mission. No one has. And it's a terrific relief to realize that you're free, free of all missions." Had someone said this to me years ago, I would have been exasperated even at the idea of it. My entire life, I was proudly raised to have very set goals and even more established plans on how to achieve those goals. Missions were a huge part of my life, and not long ago, letting go of them would have been unfathomable.

As a child or even a preteen, our so-called "missions" are usually quite simple. This makes it easy to perpetuate the idea in our minds that missions actually are useful. Perhaps if it were possible as adults to have missions as simple as those we had as children, then this reflection would be superfluous. However, as I got older, my missions seemed to flow less easily, and following through with them became more challenging. Even if I did everything

I was supposed to, my results were often not at all what I had expected. For someone like myself, who needs to have everything done and perfected in her own peculiar way, this was debilitating. It would really bother me and I would just spend—or waste, rather—way too much time figuring out what went wrong and why things didn't go my way.

After many failures, I finally realized what the problem had been all along. It was the missions themselves. My need to have everything go a certain way was an absolutely ridiculous notion. I had never taken into account that, even if everything I did on my part went well, there are many elements in our lives other than our own actions. I cannot predict what another person will do, how the traffic will flow, or even if the weather will change the next day. So how could I possibly create entire missions in life that integrate everything I need to do with supposed outcomes that I have absolutely no control over?

I realized my folly and decided to move forward with my life, but this time, with no missions at hand. At first, this was extremely difficult. I had to explain to myself that being goal-oriented was different than having entire missions to fulfill. In order to make this clearer to myself, I thought out the things that were important in my life and the possible ways to attain them. For example, I knew I wanted to succeed academically, but instead of saying, "I have to get an A this quarter," and creating an entire mission on working to get that A, I just made a pact to excel in my studying habits. If I did my assignments on time and focused when I was studying, there was little chance of not getting an A. Similarly, instead of having a grand mission for a vast community service project, I simply made a vow to be a more helpful human being from that day forward. I was able to look about and consciously help those in need around me. I still have goals; I just don't have entire missions. As a result, life has become much simpler.

Ridding myself of these missions was perhaps one of the most beneficial things I have ever done in my life. Its results were fast and amazingly fruitful. My grades shot up immediately and have never gone back down. I also discovered peace of mind and a happiness that I was unaware ever existed. Knowing that I was free of these missions really helped me live in the moment and cherish my surroundings. Living without missions has made life truly beautiful and it's a relief to be this free!

Sushana earned a bachelor's degree in art history and a minor in political science from the University of California, Los Angeles. Sushana grew up in Riverside, California, where her family still resides. Her interests include theater, traveling, reading, and cooking. She is passionate about learning about other cultures and has visited more than 20 different countries. Before attending law school, Sushana hopes to work with United Nations–sanctioned nongovernmental organizations reforming social injustices in rural South Asia.

Reach Down and Take It

by Max Baugh

I have always been somewhat of a shy person. While I'm not afraid of speaking my mind in a classroom, I have always had issues with going into new situations. On my first day of high school, I was in a regular PE class. I had been told repeatedly in the preceding few weeks that I should go out for the swim team, but when I got my schedule, there was a mix-up and I had not been placed in Sports PE. I had to go to the counselor and the swim coach to get a switch. The swim coach, Coach Anderson, was on the pool deck and the boys' water polo team was in the pool. I had a paralyzing fear of walking out onto the pool deck and looking like an idiot in front of the water polo team, so I spent over 30 minutes outside the pool deck, waiting for them to finish practice. Finally, I realized that they weren't going anywhere anytime soon, so I walked out there, only to find that the coach had already left. Fortunately, the water polo coach signed the transfer form, and I got into swimming. By the end of the

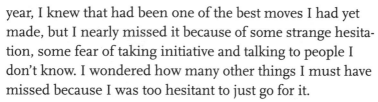

year, I knew that had been one of the best moves I had yet made, but I nearly missed it because of some strange hesitation, some fear of taking initiative and talking to people I don't know. I wondered how many other things I must have missed because I was too hesitant to just go for it.

Fyodor Dostoevsky writes in *Crime and Punishment* that "power is given only to the one who dares to reach down and take it." I think he means that a person needs to be assertive to get beyond mediocrity. The same message comes through loud and clear in Malcolm Gladwell's *Outliers*. Gladwell talks about why "natural gifts" don't have much to do with ultimate success. He asserts that he wasn't successful in college, because when he encountered problems, he never faced the challenges; he just quit.

I've been thinking that, as a first-year college student, I need to begin asserting myself more to ensure that this investment pays off. I still haven't applied the concept of reaching out and taking the power, whatever the power may be. Just mustering up the courage to knock on doors of people I don't know, to ask questions about things related to what I am trying to accomplish, seems to be a hard task for me.

But I'm trying. I'm trying to apply this principle to help bring me closer to my goal of being involved in physics research at Berkeley. One of my friends and I plan on contacting our professor from this last semester to see about either working in his lab or getting pointed in the right direction, but it is *so* intimidating to me. In our first attempt to talk with him, we got to his office door and found it shut, and there was a moment of "Should we knock? Maybe we should just leave" hesitation before, thinking of Dostoevsky's and Gladwell's messages, I knocked on the door. Unfortunately, the professor wasn't there, but it was a step in the right direction. In the last six months or so, I have been just a little more assertive as far as going out of my way to get things done.

So I am trying not to let myself miss opportunities; I am trying to set myself up to catch bigger and better opportunities. Research as a first-year student gets my foot in the door, and by the time I graduate, I hope to have done something important. I hope to get into a better graduate school as a result, leading to further opportunities, ultimately with the goal of doing something great one day.

Almost never does something great and desirable, whatever it may be, just fall out of the sky and land in someone's hand. Rather, it sits and waits to be taken by those willing to step forward and seize it. Potential doesn't really mean much if it isn't applied. This is not to say that potential has *nothing* to do with results, but rather that someone who starts with only a hint of promise can end up with far greater success if they actually apply it, using what they are initially given to manipulate the playing field in their favor.

I have come to the realization that in order to achieve what I want, I cannot sit back and assume that, because I'm a student at a top college, good things will just happen to me, because they won't. I am starting to apply the principle of reaching down and taking what I want to motivate me not to be hesitant with things, whether it's asking a question about a homework problem or getting involved in research. It's up to me to reach out, open my hand, and take hold of my dreams.

Max is majoring in physics at the University of California, Berkeley, hoping to have enough credits to graduate after only three years. He plans to spend his fourth year cramming in as many extra classes as possible, as well as doing research and maybe beginning the search for a job. His ultimate goal is to discover something that will take humanity closer to its destiny as an interstellar civilization.

Good Luck!

by Jeong Choi

Trying to boil my life philosophy down to a single quote really caused me to question and think about what it is that motivates me to continue to strive for success. It dawned on me that I hadn't given this question much thought before. I simply knew that I had zealously pursued the goals that I had set out for myself, and in achieving those goals, I had become closer to my definition of success. I was always passionate about my studies and continually strived to learn more. I was competitive by nature and had a strong desire to reach my fullest potential. These goals had driven me to where I am today. However, in order to figure out what my guiding philosophy in life was, I had to dig deeper and see what it was that underpinned these goals.

I tried to observe my daily habits and read through old academic essays and notes. I hoped to find some ideas, but I wasn't able to capture in a clear and concise quote the philosophy that motivated me in life. So I began to read some old journal entries, the earliest stretching back to middle school, and I was able to start piecing together an idea. There were notable setbacks I faced throughout these past years that I painstakingly recorded, whether it was for academic or personal reasons. My feelings of frustration were clearly written on the pages and often tinged with pessimism. Interestingly enough, I would end each of these entries not with words of defeat and hopelessness, but of resolute determination that I had the power to change my situation, whether that was how I felt or not. As I kept reading, I felt like I was getting closer to discovering what I was searching for.

I stumbled upon my answer in a rather unexpected way. While reading one of my favorite books, J.D. Salinger's *The Catcher in the Rye,* I came across something that the main character, Holden Caulfield, said that really struck me. He commented, "I'd never yell 'Good luck!' at anybody. It sounds terrible when you think about it. This is true because some people think of it as being sarcastic and also it makes it seem like you need the luck to succeed." Salinger's young protagonist brilliantly summed up my entire guiding philosophy. It all became so clear and familiar to me just what had pushed me all these years. I have never, actually, believed in luck.

"I'm just unlucky!" is a familiar expression of frustration for many of us. Whenever something doesn't go our way, we find comfort in blaming forces that are out of our control, such as fate and luck. At times, and perhaps too frequently, the success and failure of others and ourselves are attributed to these ambivalent forces. I'll easily accept that our family of origin and socioeconomic circumstances that we are born into is a matter of luck. Perhaps that these matters are the most important factors that indeed determine our future, and the notion that luck determines our fate, is a valid claim.

I strongly disagree, however, that one is hopeless in the face of certain obstacles. The moment that someone feels he has absolutely no control over the direction of his life, it seems like he relegates himself to that fate, and I have always firmly held onto the belief that, ultimately, I am the one who shapes my success or failure.

So do I believe there is a role for luck? Yes, I do, but luck is created only when I have given a task my all. Luck appears as a result of my effort to attain my fullest potential. Having the mentality that I will always strive to shape my future, even when I know that at times I do not have the capacity to control the world around me, has given me the strength to overcome challenges and persevere with a positive attitude. With each failure, there has been a lesson to be learned that has laid the foundations for my future success. As my journal entries showed, I didn't let myself get trapped into a sense of hopelessness that a frustrated mind constructs in the face of relentless challenges. I didn't give up because I simply believed I was "unlucky."

I bring about my own luck only when I have tried my best, only after I have given at least 100 percent of all I have to give. I see now that when I wish someone luck, I'm wishing for them that which lies beyond what they can do, after they have given it their all. I believe that if we combine our fullest potential with a little bit of luck, anything is possible, for any of us. And so I wish you well, I wish you the willingness to work your hardest, and I wish you a bit of good luck on your way to anything your heart desires.

Jeong graduated from University of California, Berkeley, with a degree in history. The following summer he traveled the world with his best friends. Currently, Jeong works at a broadcast media company in Seoul, South Korea, and is part of a team producing historical documentaries. He plans to attend law school in the future.

After the Spotlight

by David Hunt

Every night, I become the victim of my own restless thoughts. I am in bed, but I can't sleep. My foot is tapping. My mind is running too fast for me to keep up. I am thinking about everything that happened during the day, everything that will happen tomorrow, what I could have changed about an interaction I had months ago, and trying to figure out what the hell I am doing with my life. I know that I need to calm my mind, but I have already tried everything that I can think of and always come to the conclusion that conventional methods are of no use. The only way to slow down the stampede is to constantly remind myself of something that Richard Dawkins wrote in his book *The God Delusion*. He states, "Everything before or after the spotlight [of life] is shrouded in the darkness of the dead past, or the darkness of the unknown future." This concept helps me wrangle my thoughts and submit to the fact that I cannot hope to plan out my entire life in a single evening, nor can I fix the mistakes of my past by deconstructing them and coming up with hundreds of scenarios that could have played out differently. It all comes down to being in the present.

Currently, my thoughts have been focused on transferring out of a community college that I decided to attend primarily so that I wouldn't be a financial burden on my parents, who have been in fiscal turmoil since the beginning of my senior year of high school. In the two years I have spent there, I have become a lethargic mockery of the student I once was, because I haven't really been challenged in any of the classes I have taken. The classes seem like a waste of time that I have to fight through until the end of the semester just to give me some sense of academic connection—though at least they've kept me in school.

I now have to decide if I should stay in Southern California for college at a relatively inexpensive rate, while living at home with most of my costs paid for, but suffer the consequences of attending a school that does not offer the major, academic programs, atmosphere, or internship opportunities that I am so craving. I would still get a bachelor's degree, but it would feel cheap, like I had somehow cheated, knowing I wouldn't be learning the skills that I want to carry with me in life. The alternative is to venture out to a school that offers everything I want and more, but which is on the other side of the country and will cost about four times as much. It seems like the answer is clear, as I complain about my station of life here. In looking at the "unknown future," I see a boundless number of challenges that can present themselves in such a transition, but I also see the potential rewards that promise to outweigh any risks.

Once again, it is past midnight and I know I need to get some rest, but I also know I won't be able to sleep until I get these thoughts down on paper. I know that I don't want to be one of those people who just gets a degree for the sake of having one, and that is all that I would be accomplishing if I stayed at home. Yet I do not want to get myself into a situation that is so financially or emotionally draining that I cannot recover, either. On the other hand, I am willing to take out loans and am confident enough about my opportunities at another school that I am not daunted by the thought of struggling to get by. I am willing to face my fears of the unknown because that thought, at the end of the day, seems to be the only thing that allows me any repose. As I make this struggle black and white by putting it down on paper, it's clear to me that I am at a crossroad in my life. I am in the "darkness of the unknown future." I am certain that this will fade into the present as I choose to embrace the spotlight of my life, and as I choose to embrace the challenges I might face in the future, using them to thrust me to thrive in the present.

But for now, it is time to sleep. The spotlight will still be there in the morning.

David left home this year and transferred to the University of California, Santa Barbara, where he is pursuing a communications major with a minor in professional writing. He is in a leadership program on campus that trains guides for various outdoor activities, and he enjoys participating in and coordinating community service events whenever he can.

Life Is Always Like a Sketch

by Trent Smith

The question of whether or not life has any meaning is one that has always eaten away at me. There have been times when I have thought of life as an accident of the cause-and-effect nature of the physical universe, the simple action and reaction that plays out in everything from atoms to molecules to cells to species. In this sense, life has no meaning, and, like everything else, is simply a result of chance. With this thinking, life has no intrinsic value—only the value each of us assigns to it. Our choices are merely an extension of cause and effect, which essentially means we have no responsibility in the matter.

Another part of me, though, sees life as the most valuable thing of all. Regardless of its origins, whether the gift of physics or of God, we have been given this one life, in this one universe, and we had better make the best out of it. On the surface, this seems like the more optimistic idea, but this belief makes me uneasy as well. Though I see life as a work of art, a narrative that we write by living it, the uneasiness comes with the fact that, unlike writing in which we can make revisions, life is not so. Life is valuable, but we have only one shot at it, so we are doomed to certain failure. In this case, the sense of responsibility for our decisions becomes overwhelming.

In *The Unbearable Lightness of Being*, Milan Kundera tackles these questions in terms that make more sense to me than anything else I have encountered. He writes, "There is no means of testing which decision is better, because there is no basis for comparison. . . . And what can life be worth if the first rehearsal for life is life itself? That is why life is always like a sketch." But, as he notes, life isn't even really a sketch, for there isn't even a picture that we are drawing. Or are we?

Kundera's novel is constructed around the idea of eternal return, as posed by the philosopher Nietzsche—the possibility that everything in the universe happens over and over again in an endless cycle. If this idea is true, then it is a heavy burden we carry: we are forced to live our lives again and again, complete with all their triumphs and defeats, into eternity. If I make too many mistakes the first time, I am bound to regret life. Conversely, if life does *not* replay itself over and over like a playlist on repeat, then it takes on a quality of lightness, a sense of meaninglessness and insignificance. So I must question the ultimate value of life, either in the lightness or in the dark. In the novel, a couple, Tomás and Tereza, embodies this same contradiction. Tomás lives his life in lightness. He fears commitment, as I do, and knows that love is a decision with a heaviness that frightens him. Because he can't live life twice, he can't compare the decisions he makes with those he might have made. If he were to choose one woman, how could he possibly know she was the right choice? I, too, struggle with my choices, achingly, maddeningly, and battle over which choices are right for me.

The Unbearable Lightness of Being does not resolve the paradox of lightness versus weight. The only conclusion Kundera seems willing to draw is that the lightness of being and heaviness of being are both unbearable burdens. To me, it seems that the best route is somewhere in the middle. I tell myself that we should take life as it comes—but then, of course, I question myself. What if we let the randomness and failures in life cause us to give up on our hopes and strivings? Will life become unbearably insignificant and meaningless? On the other hand, to try to live a perfect life, to write the perfect narrative, would be a doomed endeavor that would inevitably wear us down.

So what is my conclusion to this madness? Here it is: having clear-cut answers would take all the thrill and surprise out of living. Even if life only happens once, there is enough beauty in our triumphs, and even in our failures, to make it worth our time here. I will forge ahead, weighing each choice, writing the story of my life and living it the best I can, knowing I have only this draft in front of me, and seeing what unfolds. I hope it will turn out to be a spectacular picture and an amazing read.

Trent grew up in Riverside, California, and graduated magna cum laude from the University of California, Riverside, with a bachelor of arts in creative writing. He was the 2010–2011 managing editor of UCR's Highlander *newspaper. He plans to pursue a law degree, and is currently studying for the LSAT. In his spare time, he enjoys reading and bicycling.*

Undirected

by Andi Christmas

Last month I graduated from the University of California at
Los Angeles with two bachelor's degrees. I received Highest
Departmental Honors for a thesis I wrote on 19th-century
French city planning, was inducted into the Phi Beta Kappa
Society, and my high grade-point average earned me *magna
cum laude* honors. Don't worry; the brag sheet ends here,
but I just want to illustrate that success in college does
not assure clear or simple answers. You might think that I
would be ecstatically happy and not still trying to overcome
the existential nightmare of deciding "what to be when I
grow up" and yet, at times, it seems I can think of nothing
else. Throughout my senior year, as I watched my friends
apply and get accepted to graduate programs, receive job
offers, and join exemplary organizations like the Peace
Corps and AmeriCorps, I looked on wondering exactly when
my path would reveal itself. Only in the past few weeks am

I realizing that I am the lucky one, that I have an advantage over my peers: time.

Three days after graduation, I moved halfway across the country and settled into a life where, for the first time in 16 years (18 if I count preschool), I have been neither gainfully employed nor pursuing any sort of education. This "opportunity," as I hoped to sell it to myself, has pushed me to a wide range of emotional heights: exhilaration, absolute fear, and, finally, utter relaxation. After so many years of working as hard as I could to succeed both academically and socially, I at last have unscheduled time to simply figure things out. It is a truly terrifying prospect, but one that I mean to use to the fullest.

When Steinbeck spoke of freedom in his masterpiece *East of Eden*, he referred to *timshel*, meaning "thou mayest." Timshel is the idea that we as humans are free to choose for ourselves our path to happiness and, in fact, goodness, despite obstacles we may encounter. He wrote, "And this I believe: that the free, exploring mind of the individual human is the most valuable thing in the world. And this I would fight for: the freedom of the mind to take any direction it wishes, undirected."

Though I am definitely not struggling with the same epic issues of good and evil in my own life, I am torn by a multitude of interests and potential paths. I used to view this "lack of direction" as a waste of the first quarter of my life. Now I see things differently. My indecision has given me the gift of uninterrupted time to explore each of my passions and to see each for what it truly is. With no obligation to push paper or study for eight hours a day, I am finally able to search inside myself and see what truly feels right. Will I be a teacher, an academic, a librarian, a chef, or a dancer? Will I travel the world, go back to school, or embark on some other, yet unseen, adventure?

Today, I have the freedom to explore the passions I spent years cultivating, and to seek new ones that could push me places I never thought possible. Probing these passions and transforming them into a vocation I can commit my life to is not squandering time: it is using it to the fullest. For that type of true freedom, I will fight any preconceived notion or ideology in order to find my path to happiness.

After graduating from the University of California, Los Angeles, Andi worked at the University of Chicago's Regenstein Library in the circulation department. There she learned that librarianship was not her passion but that academia was. She is enrolled in Eastern Michigan University to pursue a master's degree in history. She hopes to go on to a doctoral program and eventually teach in higher education.

You'll Move Mountains!

by I. Obi Emeruwa

It was October 31. The first snow of the year was to start that evening, just as the parents of the college's newest students were leaving. Harvard's Freshman Parents' Weekend had come to a close, and I was saying good-bye to my mother and father as they left their room at the hotel, ready to go back to California. Their departure meant a return to the anxiety that had overtaken my life. While I was settled into my room in "the Yard," as we called it, the room did not feel like home. Six weeks into my college career, I wanted nothing more than to go home—or at least to feel more at home.

Three years later, in the fall, I went for my first interview of my medical school application process, a process that has led to my current position at Columbia University. It was as if I'd traversed a seemingly insurmountable mountain that had been blocking the sun that same day three years earlier. Back on that snowy Halloween, though, you would have had a hard time convincing me that I'd ever be on the other side of the mountain, swimming in rays of sunlight, getting ready to start medical school 3,000 miles away from home.

The story of those three years is one I won't soon forget. I was reasonably certain of the path my academic career would follow at Harvard; I would study biomedical engineering and take pre-med courses, and this would lead me to a medical school somewhere in California. *The Handbook for Students* and the *Courses of Instruction* published by the Registrar's Office would be my guides to success.

As I started on my engineering courses, which were, conveniently, also some of my pre-med courses, I realized that this journey was not going to be as easy as I had expected. I especially struggled in my introductory physics mechanics course. I remember the exact grade I received on my first exam. Even more, I recall the feelings of failure and inadequacy triggered by those two digits in red ink. That struggle was a pervading theme of my freshman fall semester and the feelings that accompanied it would prove hard to shake.

It was sometime in November when I called home and spoke to my mother at length about all the things that were seemingly going wrong. I told her how I was seeing grades on exams and papers that I had never seen before, how I didn't have nearly as many friends as I had made in high school, and how I was simply unsure of what I was doing. My mother told me exactly what I needed to hear. She reminded me of the experiences that my father and she both had in college, having emigrated from Nigeria for the sole purpose of obtaining an education, leaving every single person they knew at home. My mom also reminded me about my faith; she advised me to pray and to trust God with anything that I could not fully understand myself.

With these thoughts going through my mind that autumn, it seemed less and less a coincidence to me that one of my best friends from high school had given me a copy of Dr. Seuss's *Oh! The Places You'll Go!* as a graduation gift. I had pushed myself in high school, taking some of the most demanding courses I could find. I met those challenges head-on, rarely doubting my ability to succeed. When I got to college, however, I encountered an entirely new set of obstacles. But I finally realized that Dr. Seuss was telling me what I had been hearing from my friends and family all along: "And will you succeed? Yes! You will, indeed! (98 and ¾ percent guaranteed.) KID, YOU'LL MOVE MOUNTAINS!"

After a visit home, I returned to school with a new confidence and a changed outlook. I still struggled at times, but I dealt with failure in a completely different way. I started to focus on my successes instead, and acknowledged my failures solely to learn from them. I have held on to this new outlook, especially now, as a medical student.

On October 31, 2009, I celebrated Halloween in New York City as a first-year medical student, and I reflected on the mountains that I had moved to get here. I know now that the experiences I had in college, including the ones that filled me with doubt, were key to helping me move those mountains. They changed me, instilled in me a sense of humility and ambition, and helped me grow up, while reminding me of the power and the necessity of a childlike optimism that I will carry with me no matter what mountain I next face.

Obi is pursuing his M.D. and his M.B.A. from Columbia University. His two younger sisters are also M.D. candidates at Columbia. After graduating from high school as a valedictorian, Obi earned his bachelor of arts in engineering sciences from Harvard University. He enjoys tutoring math and science, playing basketball, reading anything thought-provoking, and watching movies. He'll talk for days about medicine, education, and healthcare policy.

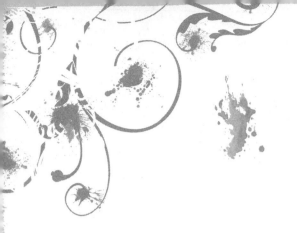

Did You Dream?

by Javier Moya

Each individual has his own driving mechanism or assortment of tools that keeps him going through a challenging ordeal, which is especially true in the military. For myself, the most prominent motivation is my dream of being a naval aviator. It would be an outstanding personal accomplishment for me to successfully go through the academy at Annapolis and dedicate part of my life to serving my country.

My parents, as immigrants, have watched four of their children go to college, but I am the first to go to a military school. I will also be the first in my family to defend our country. I have been through many mental rigors and physical tests to earn and maintain my place as a cadet. In addition to this, I am earning a position as a future officer in the United States Navy, I hope as a pilot.

Sometimes, when the mental and physical tests have drained me of all that I can give, my dreams are the only things that fuel my desire to stay at a school more rigorous than I had ever imagined a place could be. At these times, when my superiors demand more than I can put forth, I continue on even when my instincts scream at me to stop. Physical injuries and mental stress, characteristics and risks that one takes when being in such a profession, are intimidating to any newcomer entering the fraternity of the U.S. Navy.

I have watched others as bewildered as I was, facing the strenuous expectations imposed on new recruits. I had every possible justification to quit based on my own selfish impulses for comfort and not wanting to put up with overbearing authority figures. But this longing to release myself from this commitment contradicted the dreams I had of what I wished to accomplish. Additionally, I had those whom I considered family, a home away from home, and we had put our faith and trust in one another to see this endeavor through to the end. My classmates and I had the extra incentive of mutual desire to accomplish our goals and see our dreams come true, and I'm grateful for this. Without them, I am certain that quitting might have been an option for me.

To describe my time here at the Naval Academy, I can easily call forth a line from Aldous Huxley's *Brave New World,* when one of the characters asks his companion, "And did you dream of anything?" He answers like I would, and says that his dream entailed a great sacrifice, but one that was worth giving his life for, simply because he was called to experience the ultimate sacrifice. And for me, serving my country is this type of ultimate sacrifice.

I couldn't possibly be here if I had not had a dream at some point—a goal that could be fulfilled by attending this institution. My ability to pursue and achieve my dreams at this institution will be worth everything I have to give up in the process. The physical training has been unforgiving and the academic workload unlike that of any other school I had considered. What I wish to do in the future, however, can be accomplished only by being a member of the United States Naval Academy Brigade of Midshipmen. My experience here is almost like a dream come true in itself, for I had dreamed of going to a great college, but at one time I did not think it was possible for me to be in a service academy or accepted into one of the most prestigious institutions in the nation. And yet, here I am.

It was the dream of what could be that motivated me to continue the effort even when the odds were against me. It is when there is nothing left that one must think back to dreams and the aspirations within them, calling upon them to continue and persevere until the objective is met—and then push onward to raise the bar even further. With these highest of ideals, it will be an honor to see my dream come to fruition as I serve my country.

Javier is the youngest of four children, the fourth in his family to go to college, but the first to attend a service academy. He will graduate from Annapolis in the class of 2012, with aviation as a service specialty preference. He enjoys chess and astronomy. He will be commissioned as a second lieutenant in the U.S. Navy and will proudly serve his country with honor.

And So...

Questions for Reflection, Discussion, and Writing

As a young person, you may often have heard the message that the "world is your oyster"—that your life can be anything you imagine, dream, or aspire to make of it. The future can be exciting and scary at the same time. It holds amazing possibilities as well as tremendous challenges for all of us. A life without goals can seem to be also without purpose—yet, with too many expectations, you could easily find yourself despairing when your goals seem out of reach. As you reflect on this section's essays on goals, think about how you relate to what the writers have experienced. What are *your* hopes and dreams? How do you envision your future, and how is that vision shaped by your past?

In *Quentin's* essay, she explores her discovery of her passions and goals. What are your ideas about how you'd like to spend your life? What has influenced these desires and dreams? Quentin also notes the first book that she fell in love with. Can you recall the first book you really enjoyed? Why did it resonate with you so deeply? Do you still feel the same about it as you did the first time you read it?

Hongyu brings up the subject of pride. Many times, our pride and our competitive natures can keep us from being satisfied with our progress. Think about a time when you were like Hongyu and your pride got in your way, or you would have rather given up everything than be content with the measure of success you *did* have. Would you do things differently if you had another chance?

Sushana notes that the idea of a mission became overused in her own life. Name a "mission" that you hope to achieve. Then, instead of focusing on this large goal, list the little, day-by-day activities and characteristics you'll need to reach your goal. How do you think you'll feel if you succeed? What if you fall short, but find new "missions" along the way?

As *Max* points out, sometimes it can be hard to ask for—or demand—the things we want or need. Discuss a time when you desperately wanted something, but obstacles kept you from reaching your goal. What dreams do you have that require you to get outside of your comfort zone and ask for help or direction? What could you do today to move closer to these goals or aspirations?

Trent goes back and forth about light and dark, positive and negative, noting that there is no clear answer when trying to figure out how best to live his life. Do you have this kind of inner struggle with uncertainty about how to approach your life and pursue your dreams, or do you feel confident about the road you're on? Consider the ways you've decided what your goals are and how they've changed over time.

David is struggling with the major life decision of whether to stay at home or go away to college. What are some of the toughest choices you've had to make in your life? Does leaving home, or doing something else in which you have no idea of the outcome, scare you or excite you? Write about some of your own options for your future. Try to be as specific as possible when weighing the pros and cons of each choice. How do you go about making difficult decisions?

Jeong considers the ideas of luck, destiny, and hard work. How do you view these ideas? Do you know people who work very hard but face challenges that block them from moving forward, while others seem to sail easily through life? Explain how your beliefs about free will, fate, destiny, and luck influence how you live your life. Jeong also reflects on what his past journal entries revealed to him or reminded him of. Have you ever kept a journal? If so, what kinds of patterns have you noticed in your old entries? How have your beliefs changed—or stayed the same—over time?

Andi gives her "résumé" at the beginning of her essay, and then admits that, after all she had achieved, it still wasn't *everything* to her. How do you explain who you are to people? Do you tend to list qualities or achievements that you think will impress others? If so, how does this affect the way you set goals for yourself, or the way you view the future? Have you ever made a point of focusing on the present? If so, how did that affect your outlook?

The words of a favorite childhood author remind *Obi* that anything is possible in his life. As a kid, what was your favorite book or author? Choose one childhood story and consider the life lessons in it that are still meaningful to you. Explain how that book or story might help you face challenges and live your life with more knowledge and peace.

What do you dream? *Javier* asks himself that question in his essay. Ask yourself the same thing: What do you long for in your life and your future? What do you hope to see and learn and experience along this journey? What do you hope to contribute to this world, or leave for those who will follow in your footsteps?

Using This Book with Students

A Guide for Teachers and Leaders

As noted in the introduction, C.S. Lewis was quoted as saying, "We read to know we are not alone." Additionally, I believe that we *write* to know we are not alone. In the process of reflecting on what we have read, and then committing our own thoughts to the written word, we connect with the greater world around us.

Your students write papers for school, essays for standardized tests, and essays for college credit. They may also be preparing to write personal essays for college applications and scholarships. The essays, prompts, and ideas in *Bookmarked* offer a great place to begin this process. Use the following suggestions to guide, inspire, and strengthen your students' writing. Many of these ideas can, with slight modifications, work well with a group or with individuals. Do what works best for you and the young people you work with.

Anchor Students' Writing and Your Group's Discussion

The ideas, literary works, and questions from *Bookmarked* are great springboards for students to use in their own personal writing. They also provide good starting points for wide-ranging discussions with your group. But eventually, no matter where the discussion drifts to, always bring it back to the foundational text. I call this "anchoring" the reading or writing. The key is having a thorough knowledge of your text (novel, short story, poem, essay), knowing who your students are, and being willing to make an authentic connection between life and literature. The details of a curriculum—the tests, language, mechanics, or plots—may fade from students' memories in 10 years. What will remain vivid, however, are the lessons they carry away from the literature they've read, as well as the insightful discussions they've had in class. The ways in which books mark our lives becomes the foundation—the anchor—for teaching literature and writing.

- Invite your students to use the essays from *Bookmarked* as models for this kind of anchored writing. Have each student choose one of the book's 50 essays and treat it as a foundation text for his or her own essay, analyzing the piece and exploring its ideas.

- Work with students on how to integrate quotes into their own writing. Sometimes writers randomly "drop" quotes into their text to give authority to their writing. Choose several essays to serve as examples, and use only the section of each essay that incorporates the quote. Talk with students about how these writers use the quotes effectively, and how they integrate them with their own writing.

- Ask each student to bring in a quote that best embodies his or her way of looking at the world. Although you could suggest it comes only from poetry or a book, you might open it up to *any* type of written word: a song lyric, a line from one of their poems or a friend's poem, or even something they read in a blog or elsewhere online. Encourage them to explore whether *who* wrote or said the quote matters to them. Does knowing the identity of an author make a message more authentic or important, or are the words equally meaningful no matter where or who they originated from?

• Volunteer to share some of your own written work with the group, and talk about how you anchored this particular piece. Often, young writers don't realize that *all* of us have trouble putting pen to paper and accurately presenting our intimate thoughts in a clear and grounded way. When they see you sharing your work, they will gain a more meaningful understanding of this aspect of the writing process, and they'll also learn more about the importance of anchoring their own writing. In addition, sharing on this level can help establish great trust between you and your students.

Be Authentic

Be authentic, on all levels, as often as you possibly can be. Find ways to make genuine connections with your students. Maybe you can do this by finding a band you and a student both like, by sharing a personal story of hardship or growth, or by being willing to admit you don't know the answer to a question. After all, we are all still students on a lifelong path of learning. Acknowledging this truth is an essential part of being a great teacher. Encourage this same authenticity from your students in their writing and in group discussions. Use the following ideas for sparking open, honest, and authentic conversation or writing.

• Have each student choose one of the "And So . . ." prompts and read it aloud. Discuss students' answers to these questions, or invite them to write essays in response.

• Choose an essay from the book and have students read it aloud, taking turns. Then ask them to reflect on the essayist's experience, message, and voice as a writer.

Encourage discussion of how using tone and language in different ways can convey different feelings and moods. Also note that the way we look at situations can sometimes be more about choice and attitude than circumstance. Gently push students to suggest alternative ways these writers might have looked at their challenges and how their essays—and their lives—might have been different if they had done so.

- Choose one quote from *Bookmarked* and have students freewrite in response to it, without holding back or editing their writing. After a set amount of time, invite those who feel comfortable to share what they have written.

Connect Students' Outside World to the World Inside the Classroom

Work to make your classroom current and to incorporate technology into your activities. Most students use Facebook, texting, Twitter, and other forms of technology to keep in touch. By incorporating these forms of communication into everyday assignments, and then helping students translate this into a more formal standard of writing and speaking, you help them bridge the gap between academic language and their more familiar colloquial communication.

- Select a quote from one of the essays in *Bookmarked* and ask every student to write it at the top of a sheet of paper. Then let students "blog" on the quote, using colloquial language to express their thoughts. After a few minutes, have students pass the papers to someone else and continue writing, adding to the new hard copy blogs in front of them. Afterward, make copies of these blogs and send them home with students, asking them to use more formal and academic language to summarize the conversation. If you like, use the at-home writing as a jumping-off point for discussion the next day.

- Suggest that students create text-message conversations between themselves and one of the student-writers in *Bookmarked*. Suggest that they respond to the essay with their own thoughts, experiences, or feedback, and that they pretend the essayist is a friend. Then ask them to imagine what the essay writer would text back, and write down both sides of this imagined conversation. (This could also be an interesting conversation to compose with a fictional character from a piece you're reading in class.) Encourage students to think about the nature of texting as a form of communication. What, if anything, gets lost in translation when writing this way?

- Have students find "matching" quotes from any genre— song lyrics, poetry, a commercial, a news article, etc.— embodying the same messages or overriding themes as quotes from essays in *Bookmarked*. Discuss the quotes as a group, or have students write essays comparing and contrasting them.

- Ask students to create imaginary Facebook pages for characters from a book they are reading. (They could do this in hard copy or on a class website.) What fan groups is this character part of? Who are his or her friends? You could also ask students to list the last 20 websites that their chosen characters might have visited. It would be interesting to see what Jay Gatsby, Harry Potter, or Jane Eyre would have in their search engine histories!

Be Open to Students Becoming Authorities on Their Own Writing Process

Because students tend to see their teachers as the authority on writing, they often overlook their own ability to critique their own writing. Strengthen their voices and confidence as writers and readers with the following activities.

- Ask students to produce their own prompts based on the essays in *Bookmarked,* or based on the texts you are reading in class, and to write essays in response. Then invite the group to grade or edit one another's pieces in a respectful and constructive way. By doing this as a class, students begin to take ownership over their own writing process. They start to see how everyone has something to offer as both a writer and an editor.

- Ask students to choose issues (for example, social, political, personal) raised in essays found in *Bookmarked* and then put them in charge of running Socratic seminars on their topics. When the students become the teachers for a day and take ownership of their learning, they often find ways to approach ideas that you might have overlooked in your own perspective of the curriculum. They also gain confidence as leaders, make important connections with their peers, and strengthen their skills as thoughtful readers and writers.

- Bring in a selection of meaningful or interesting quotes that are connected to something you're reading as a group, and invite students to bring in some of their own. Share all of the quotes in a handout and ask everyone to privately pair each quote with a classmate they think embodies those words in some way. (Require students to be respectful and considerate throughout this activity.) After some time, start sharing quotes as a class, asking students to make a note of the quotes they're "assigned" without discussion for the time being. Then, have the kids take the quotes home and spend some time reflecting on these words' relevance to themselves and their lives. Revisit the activity with a discussion the next day and see where the conversation goes. By keeping the quotes positive in nature, this activity can help students understand more clearly the value others see in them.

Be Courageous—Find New Ways of Approaching an Old Idea

Creative, innovative projects can help make literature relevant to your students in new and meaningful ways. Try any of the following ideas and add your own. Follow up by having students talk and write about the experience, how it made them feel, and what they learned about life, literature, and themselves in the process. All of these activities give students a glimpse of what these characters experienced, teaching them empathy toward the hardships of others. This empathy, in turn, infuses into their personal writing, giving a voice to their own experiences.

- Read a work of literature explored in one of the essays in *Bookmarked* and then create a class project that connects the work with real life. For example, ask students to wear letters around their necks, exposing whatever they view as their worst character defects, just as Hester Prynne had to in *The Scarlet Letter*. Or challenge them to go a week without any luxuries (no technology, changing clothes, fast food) when they read *The Grapes of Wrath*. Another idea is to have students make their own boxes of precious things they would save if they suffered through a fire, as Miss Maudie did in *To Kill a Mockingbird*.

- Keeping a journal of one's life integrates the outer self with the more intimate self. Encourage each and every student to practice writing on a regular basis, not for a grade or for your class, but for themselves. If someone discovers something about himself or herself through this writing process and wants to share it, you could create an online file-sharing system or another way for students to discuss their writing, feelings, and epiphanies with their peers. This personal writing and sharing is never to be regimented or required, just gently used as a reminder that each of us has an inner writer waiting to be heard.

- Often we ask our students to write "something original," but give them limited suggestions for *how* to make their writing unique, fresh, and interesting. Help them find their voices by reminding them to find the beauty in ugliness, see the unique in the mundane, and elaborate on the lessons they have learned versus just the challenges they have faced, intertwining these all into a story that only they can tell and call their own.

Be Clear About Your Writing Expectations for Your Students

Require students to write their own essays. Period. Remind them that no matter how tempting it may be to use those websites that allow someone else to do the work for them, it's cheating, plain and simple. Writing a personal essay for college will be one of the most important challenges faced by students who choose the path of higher education. They will have to paint a clear picture, in 1,000 words or less, of themselves, their backgrounds, their resilience to life's hardships, and some unique aspect that makes them a solid fit for a particular college. In other words, they will have a chance to tell their story. They will benefit, therefore, from exercises and activities that excavate their innermost ideologies, values, and identities.

- Have your students practice using others' words as a springboard but not a script. Following the model of the essays in *Bookmarked*, ask students to choose quotes from literature that embody their own life philosophies, personalities, fears, dreams, or any other aspects of themselves. Then invite them to write original, personal essays about how these words have influenced them, touched their souls, and become part of the fabric of their character.

- Talk with students about the fact that plagiarism isn't always as obvious as a paragraph or two copied verbatim from another source. Using someone else's key thesis without attribution or "borrowing" even a handful of phrases can tarnish the reputation of a talented author or lead to the rejection of an otherwise good piece of writing. As a class or in small groups, discuss various aspects of plagiarism and the limitations and/or consequences that it can bring, academically, professionally, and personally.

- One foundational part of writing is gathering word choices and ideas from varying sources. Ask students to list the many places one can gather sources of information and ideas. Then, establish *how* to translate all of this into original writing. Choose paragraphs from the essays in *Bookmarked* and ask the students to rewrite the paragraphs *in their own words*. Ask them to examine any confusion they might have had when they were leaning toward copying even a word or a concept from the original essay. Discuss ways to reach beyond this "writer's block," such as using a thesaurus, having a discussion with a peer, or seeking input from a parent or teacher.

- Find an article or blog that embodies a general theme that teens might face. Ask them to rewrite the section of writing *in their own words*. Then, in small groups, have students share their writing with one another and see if any two rewrites sound alike. This is a good way to highlight the overuse of common phrases and to point out that, although ideas can be similar, students' writing must be original.

Think Outside the Book

Writing a strong personal essay means tapping into deep feelings and conveying them in a clear, powerful way. Invite your students to go beyond literature in search of this kind of personal writing, and encourage them to write from the heart about themselves and their lives.

- Ask your students to write about scars they may have on their bodies. Encourage them to explore the circumstances behind their scars, and to elaborate on other things that were going on in their lives at the time. Then ask them to write about the scars that are *not* seen, the ones on their hearts and souls. Invite them to explore how they have healed from these wounds and how their scars have changed them as people. (*Note:* If a student writes about being abused or about self-harm, *do not ignore this information.* Follow your school's policy guidelines on mandatory reporting.)

- Find a picture, of anything, and ask students to write about how their own life circumstances relate to the picture. The image can be of a person, place, or thing, but this activity often works best with an abstract piece. It's amazing to see the connections students make to these illustrations.

- Ask your group to answer Shakespeare's question: "What's in a name?" Do your students like their names? Are there stories behind how they got their names? Would they ever change their names, and, if so, to what? Then discuss how making this change might change other people's view or perception of them.

- Invite students to think about defining gifts they've received sometime in the past. Ask them to explore how these gifts reflected or represented their personalities, hopes, desires, values, or even fears. Why were these gifts so important to them? They could also reflect on gifts that they longed for but never received, and what the importance was of these particular "un-given" gifts. Then have them form small groups and share their thoughts with one another. Consider asking each group to compose a group poem about gifts—both those received and not received—and to share this poem with the rest of the class.

A Note from the Editor

In closing, I commend each of you, as dedicated educators, and your work, which so often goes unnoticed and without glory. You make an indelible mark on your students' lives with your words of authentic praise, your connections with students as individuals, and your courage to be bold and do things a little differently than other teachers might. Holding your student-writers to high standards shows them that you believe in their worth and their ability to reach beyond anything they might have imagined for themselves. By helping them find, tell, and write their own stories, you are helping them leave a path for others to follow, just as the essayists in *Bookmarked* have done. Thank you for the work you do each day.

Ann Camacho

Index of Authors

Index of Works

Index

Acknowledgments

Though your name may not appear below, I am grateful to all of those who have shared their stories, their hearts, and their support with me over the years. Teaching has been a gift for me, and I have always said that I've learned as much as I have ever taught.

I do have special thanks to offer, of course. First, and foremost, to Jessica Trumble and Adam Fletcher, my student-editors, who not only wrote their own essays for this book but also spent countless hours poring over these stories, reading each word with the intent of keeping every student's voice clear and authentic. To my principal of 19 years, Dale Kinnear, who through his mentoring and support has given me wings to soar. To MaryAnn Solorzano, a friend and colleague who championed my idea and believed in my ability to bring this book to fruition. To my dear friend April Lidinsky, a professor and author who was the best cheerleader a writer could have. To Columbia professor Edward Mendelson for giving me his valuable time and feedback. To Gayle Brandeis, a brilliant writer, for always showing grace and humility, and suggesting I turn a noun into a verb. To Inlandia Institute, Marion, Cati, and all the dedicated staff. I am forever grateful for their love of the written word. To Donna, who always seems to have just the right words. To Carol, whose guidance as a writing coach was invaluable. To my dear friends, especially Montie, Brenda, Connie, Brandina, Paris, Maria, Katja, and Anne, who believed in me and this book even when I had my doubts. To Jim and Trish, my surrogate parents, whose love and counsel have sustained me over the years. To Ashleigh, Tamara, and Eric, for always caring for and loving my girls when I had to be away. To Jeremy, for rescuing me from my many computer glitches. To Darren, for giving me the Back-to-the-Grind coffee house, a perfect place for grading and writing.

To my sister, my mother, and my father, who loved me and instilled in me my love of education—I love you. To Marvin, for watching over and loving our girls while I spent countless hours working on the minute details of these inspiring essays. Thank you for your belief in my dream. To my daughters, for sharing my time and attention while I poured myself into this project. I hope you will see, in this book, a bigger gift: the courage to always follow your own path and dreams. I love you both with my whole heart.

To those at Free Spirit Publishing, for taking on this manuscript and seeing the wisdom and beauty these students' stories had to offer, especially Alison Behnke, my editor, who always took into consideration my concerns, issues, changes, and revisions. Thank you, also, to designer Michelle Lee and publicist Elena Meredith for their creativity and commitment, which helped bring this book to life. I hope all authors experience the same kind of patience and gentle guidance through the daunting undertaking of the writing process.

And finally, to every student who submitted an essay, whether it appears in this book or not: Thank you for your willingness to bare your soul, step up with courage and effort, and share your story with me. There are no words to tell you the gratitude and admiration I have for all of you as integral parts of my teaching story. You took on my invitation without questioning the integrity with which I would use your essays, showing unwavering trust. Most of all, I stand in awe of the amazing young people you have become. Without you, none of this would have been possible.

About the Editor

Ann Camacho grew up in Lakewood, Colorado. She earned her master's equivalent in secondary education from the University of Denver, and her master's degree in English from National University. She has also earned Advanced Placement and International Baccalaureate (IB) certification. Ann has taught for over 20 years, most of them at John W. North High School in Riverside, California. She has taught all levels, from English as a second language to Honors American Literature, IB/Pre-AP. The IB curriculum is intellectually challenging, with an emphasis on a global perspective. Advanced Placement classes serve as valuable preparation for college courses.

Ann also teaches AVID (Advancement Via Individual Determination) classes. AVID's goal is to close the achievement gap and to prepare all students for college and beyond. The program serves over 400,000 students across the nation. Ann has attended six of the AVID Summer Institute programs in San Diego.

Ann loves to read, have philosophical conversations, watch great dramas and romantic comedies, and find treasures in antique stores. Teaching has been her life's passion and has been surpassed only by the time she spends raising her two girls. Though Ann loves traveling to faraway lands and learning about other people and customs, she is also content being a homebody, spending time with family and friends. She hopes to make a difference in the world through teaching literature, one book at a time.

Other Great Books from Free Spirit

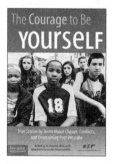
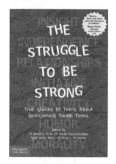